BARCODE IN BACK

Wawatay

Wawatay

Penny Gummerson

Playwrights Canada Press
Toronto • Canada

Playwrights Canada Press
The Canadian Drama Publisher
215 Spadina Avenue, Suite 230, Toronto, Ontario CANADA M5T 2C7
416-703-0013   fax 416-408-3402
orders@playwrightscanada.com • www.playwrightscanada.com

Financial support provided by the taxpayers of Canada and Ontario through the Canada Council for the Arts and the Department of Canadian Heritage through the Book Publishing Industry Development Programme, and the Ontario Arts Council.

Front cover photo "Aurora over Vee Lake, near Yellowknife" by Yuichi Takasaka
Production Editor/Cover design: JLArt

Library and Archives Canada Cataloguing in Publication

Gummerson, Penny
    Wawatay / Penny Gummerson.

A play.
ISBN 0-88754-780-X

    I. Title.

PS8613.U52W38 2005   C812'.6   C2005-903864-0

First edition: July 2005.
Printed and bound by AGMV Marquis at Quebec, Canada.

*Dedicated to my mom, Joyce Gummerson,
who continues to guide and inspire me
from the Spirit World.*

Kisakgihitin, Nikawiy.

Awards

Wawatay won the Vancouver Jessie Richardson Theatre Award for Outstanding Original Play, 2002. It was also nominated for Best Production, Sydney Risk Award for Outstanding Original Script by an Emerging Playwright, Best Director and Best Actor.

Wawatay was a Stage-Play Finalist in the Moondance International Film Festival, Denver, Colorado, 2002.

Wawatay won the People's Choice Favourite New Play Award at the Vancouver New Play Festival, 2001.

Penny Gummerson won a Playwright's Theatre Centre/Jessie Richardson Theatre Award for Most Promising New Playwright, 2001.

Acknowledgements

Hy Hy Manitou.

Thanks to my family—Dad, Sue, Cathy, Bob, Don, Barb, Jen, Ken, Max, Georgia, Danny and Colleen—for their love and support.

Heartfelt thanks to my dramaturge, Chapelle Jaffe, for her undying support, encouragement and keen dramaturgical eye.

Thanks also to Jill Williams and Anne Anglin for their notes on earlier drafts.

Thanks to the many actors, directors, crew, artistic directors and staff who were a part of workshops and productions at the Firehall Arts Centre (Vancouver), Playwrights Theatre Centre (Vancouver), Native Earth Performing Arts (Toronto), Saskatchewan Native Theatre Company (Saskatoon) and the Northwest First Nations Theatre Collective (Terrace, B.C.).

Hy Hy to Elder Bernice Hammersmith, Elders Phil and Giselle L'Hirondelle, Elder Aline LaFlamme and Elder Pauline Johnson for sharing their teachings so freely.

Thanks to the Canada Council for the Arts and the City of Vancouver for their financial support.

Playwright's Notes/Introduction

When my mom died in 1995 it shook my world. It was a painful time. The night before her funeral, *Wawatay* lit up the northern skies in my hometown of Flin Flon, Manitoba. My brother, Don, and I sat in his truck and watched them dance over a white blanket of freshly fallen snow. "A ballet from Heaven." We watched in silence. I turned to him and said, "Mom's going to a good place." He smiled and nodded. My journey of healing began in that moment. Two years later, I started to write *Wawatay*. Four years later, I finished it. *Wawatay* is a story about family pain, shame and secrets. It is also a story of healing and hope. It is my hope that this play brings good medicine to your heart.

All My Relations,

Penny E. Gummerson (Oomeemew Iskwew)

Setting

Flin Flon, Manitoba. A small, northern Canadian community. Spring is just around the corner, snow is still on the ground.

Act One takes place in a Catholic hospital and Jaz's Vancouver apartment. There are seven different settings in the hospital: 1.) Lois's Hospital Room, 2.) Waiting Room, 3.) Chapel, 4.) Cafeteria, 5.) Park Bench (outside hospital), 6.) Doctor's Office Door, 7.) Pay phone.

Act Two takes place in, and around, the family home. The home is surrounded by bush and a lake is nearby. There are seven different settings: 1.) Lois's Bedroom, 2.) Living Room, 3.) Dining Area, 4.) Mary's Altar (in the living room), 5.) Porch Steps, 6.) Jaz's Stump/Backyard 7.) Hanging Tree (near Jaz's stump).

Production Notes

Jaz's stump (in backyard) and Mary's altar (in living room) are directly opposite each other.

A real eagle feather is not used in the production of this play.

Music: A CD of the songs is available from the author for production purposes only.

Lighting

Lighting levels are integral in bringing this play to life. Throughout the duration of *Wawatay*, the audience will see ALL of the characters, ALL of the time. Meaning, the action is concurrent. The actors will move through space—like butterflies—floating from one setting to another. Soft lights will be on the characters at all times, however, stronger lighting will be used to emphasise which character we are focusing on at particular points throughout the play.

Time

Present. The action of the play takes place over one week.

Production Information

Wawatay premiered in February 2002 at the Firehall Arts Centre, Vancouver, B.C. with the following company:

FRANK	Jay Brazeau	JUNIOR	Tracey Olson
BJ	Marcus Hondro	MARY	Suzanne Ristic
JAZ	Cheri Maracle	LOIS	Susan Ringwood

Directed by Donna Spencer
Stage Management by John James Hong
Costume Design by Barbara Clayden
Set Design by Adam Parboosingh
Lighting Design by James Proudfoot
Sound Design and Musical Compositions by Russell Wallace
Lyrics by Penny Gummerson
Cree Translation by Elder Bernice Hammersmith

•••

Wawatay received its second production with the Saskatchewan Native Theatre Company in Saskatoon, Saskatchewan, May 2003, directed by Alanis King. Its third production was with the Northwest First Nations Theatre Collective in Terrace, B.C. in February 2004, directed by Marianne Weston.

•••

Wawatay received several workshops:
Weesageechak Begins to Dance Festival, Native Earth Performing Arts Theatre, Toronto, Ontario, November 2000, directed by Anne Anglin.
Vancouver New Play Festival, Playwright's Theatre Centre, Vancouver, B.C., May 2001, directed by Kathryn Bracht.
Firehall Arts Centre in Vancouver, B.C., October 2001, sponsored by the Vancouver Playwrights Theatre Centre, directed by Donna Spencer.

Characters

JAZ: Youngest daughter. Age 30. Free-spirited artist. Long, dark hair. The only one to embrace her Native roots. The black sheep of the family. Hasn't been home in ten years.

LOIS: The dying mother. 60. Petite. Gentle-looking. The glue that has held this family together for 40-odd years.

FRANK: The father. Half-Cree Indian, but passes for "white." Age 65. Retired. Patriarch. Loves his wife. Has denied his Native roots his entire adult life.

MARY: Eldest daughter. Age 42. Super-responsible. Level-headed. A staunch Catholic. Desperately wants children, but can't get pregnant.

BJ: Eldest son. Age 40. Loves hunting and trapping. Handsome. A great storyteller. Peacemaker. Recovering alcoholic.

JUNIOR: Younger son. Age 38. An executive. Loves money. Despite a good education, a racist. Angry. A drinker. His father's favourite.

Cree Translation

Elder Bernice Hammersmith

Wawatay

Act One

JAZ's Vancouver apartment. In the dark, a smudge bowl burns. Pow wow music plays. Lights up. Soft spot reveals JAZ smudging. She cups the smoke over her head, face and heart, then starts dancing the "Fancy Shawl Dance." Her hair is in braids, a choker of beaded strips or bone hair pipes around her neck. She is dressed in traditional Fancy Dance regalia—bright-coloured cloth dress with matching high-top moccasins, a brightly-coloured shawl over her shoulders with elaborate designs, appliqué, ribbon work, and painting; a vest under the shawl and/or the large collar over the shawl. Long fringe hangs from the edges of the shawl, and flies around as she sallies forth.

This dance is quite athletic. Fast, intricate footwork, combined with jumping and spinning, while keeping time with the music. The dance style mimics butterflies in flight—playful, graceful and light.

This is JAZ's vision. It is not the first time she has had a vision or experienced visions of her mother. She has always had a special relationship with her mother and is very connected to her on a spirit plane. She is, however, very concerned when her mother appears in this particular vision—she knows something's wrong.

As JAZ dances, a soft spot comes up on a hospital room. LOIS, dressed in a long, white gown, lies in the hospital bed. Beside the bed—an IV unit, respirator, heart machine. Above the bed, hangs a cross. MARY, clutching a rosary, sits in a chair next to her mother and prays. Unbeknownst to MARY, LOIS gets out of the hospital bed and walks toward JAZ. MARY continues to pray. LOIS smiles and watches JAZ dance. Lights fade on LOIS. JAZ continues to dance. On another part of the stage, LOIS appears again. JAZ continues dancing. LOIS appears again—this time, she holds out her arms to JAZ, beckoning her. JAZ stops dancing. She stares at her mother. LOIS walks from JAZ's "vision" back to the hospital bed. She climbs in and hooks herself up to the machines ie., IV, heart monitor, respirator. The respirator starts to hiss.

As LOIS hooks herself up to machines, JAZ walks over to her stereo and turns off the pow wow music. She picks up a framed photo of her mother from a table and stares at it. She puts the photo down and exits.

As lights fade on hospital room and JAZ's apartment, lights come up on the other side of the stage: waiting area, Catholic hospital. A crucifix hangs on the wall. There is a couch, several chairs, coffee table littered with magazines and a water cooler. FRANK paces waiting area. Beat.

BJ and JUNIOR enter. JUNIOR is dressed in a suit and tie, long dress coat. He carries a briefcase. BJ is unshaven, wearing stained jeans, muddy boots, checkered bush jacket and a baseball cap. He carries a canvas pack.

JUNIOR   Hey, Pops.

FRANK   Where the hell have you two been?

JUNIOR   How's Ma?

FRANK   *(to BJ)* Jee-zuz! You look like you just crawled out of the bloody bush!

JUNIOR   He did.

BJ   We got here as fast as we could. How's Mom?

FRANK   She's got an infected leg!

JUNIOR   How the hell did that happen?

BJ   Where is she?

FRANK   *(pointing with his lips)* In there.

   BJ heads for curtained-off area.

JUNIOR   She didn't say anything to me about a sore leg.

FRANK	You know your mother— *(to BJ)* Where the hell do you think you're going?
BJ	*(stopping)* To see Mom.
FRANK	*(loudly)* Go wash your hands first. And take off that goddamn cap. We're in a hospital, eh? And be quiet. Mary said to be quiet.
BJ	Sure, Dad.

BJ exits. FRANK calms down, becomes quieter.

FRANK	Jee-zus, he stinks like a muskrat in heat. Who's he think he is, comin' in here covered in goddamn dirt and germs?
JUNIOR	He wanted to stop and get cleaned up. I'm the one who told him we didn't have time.
FRANK	Well—Christ! Does he live on that bloody trapline or what?
JUNIOR	What the hell happened to her, Dad?

MARY leaves LOIS's room. FRANK sits. JUNIOR sits beside him.

FRANK	We're watching "Canada AM" and I get up to get me another coffee, eh. I tap her toe with my cup—just gently, mind you—and, Christ, you'd think I'd belted her with a two by four. She screamed bloody murder. I say how long's that foot of yours been hurtin' you?…

MARY enters waiting room and starts talking to JUNIOR. FRANK continues to tell his story to JUNIOR, but JUNIOR isn't listening to him. He's more concerned with what MARY has to say. MARY and JUNIOR's conversation overlaps FRANK's story of what happened.

MARY	*(overlapping FRANK, to JUNIOR)* Good. You're here. Where's BJ?
FRANK	…she says: "About a week." A whole goddamn week! Jeezus Christ, she could barely walk.
JUNIOR	*(overlapping FRANK)* Gone to wash up. How's Mom?
FRANK	…Had to carry her to the car. And you know what she says to me? She says…

MARY	*(overlapping FRANK)* She's doing just… fine.
JUNIOR	*(overlapping FRANK)* Doesn't sound like it to me.
FRANK	*(to JUNIOR and MARY)* For chrissakes, am I talkin' to the air, here? Hey, anybody listenin' to me?

Beat. They both look at FRANK.

MARY	*(to JUNIOR)* They've got her on a Heparin drip now.
JUNIOR	What the hell's that supposed to mean?
FRANK	Watch your mouth. We're in a hospital, eh?

MARY makes the sign of the cross. BJ enters.

BJ	*(to MARY)* How is she?
MARY	The nurses are doing everything they can for her.
BJ	What's wrong with her leg?
MARY	They found a blood clot.

JUNIOR and BJ respond at the same time.

JUNIOR	A blood clot!?
BJ	A blood clot!?
FRANK	For chrissakes, keep it down!
MARY	Heparin's a blood-thinner. It'll remove the clot. Eventually.
JUNIOR	Whaddya mean, eventually?
FRANK	Her leg's swollen like a tree stump. The doctor said it could take a while.
JUNIOR	How long's a while? A couple of days? A week?
MARY	They don't know, Junior.
BJ	I want to see her.
MARY	She's sleeping.
BJ	That's okay. I just want to see her.
FRANK	She's asleep, goddamnit!

MARY   (*calming FRANK*) It's okay, Dad. (*to BJ*) They've got her hooked up to a bunch of machines, Beej. But they're just monitors, that's all. Nothing to be alarmed about.

BJ nods. He heads for LOIS's bed and stops.

BJ   (*to JUNIOR*) You comin'?

JUNIOR   I… well. I uh… don't think it's such a good idea if we're all in there at once. Crowdin' her and everything. I'll just wait here with Dad.

BJ   Suit yourself.

BJ exits to LOIS's bed. He stares at all the machines, runs his hands along the tubes. He takes off his ball cap and sits on the chair beside his LOIS's bed.

MARY looks at FRANK and JUNIOR.

MARY   I'll be right back.

MARY exits to hospital chapel. She crosses herself, kneels and prays.

FRANK   I hate the smell of these goddamn hospitals. They can scrub the floors all they want to. It still stinks of piss to me!

JUNIOR   Mare seems to think they pretty much got everything under control.

FRANK   She's just puttin' on a good face. Like her mom.

JUNIOR   What do you mean?

FRANK   Your mother's foot is the size of a goddamn football.

JUNIOR   That's because of the clotting, Dad. Once the medication starts working—

FRANK   It looks more like gangrene to me.

JUNIOR   Gangrene?

FRANK   I don't think they're tellin' us everything they know.

JUNIOR   Come on, Dad. They would have told us if it was gangrene!

FRANK   I've seen it before. It looks just like that.

JUNIOR   Dad, it's not gangrene.

> *Beat. JUNIOR thinks about it.*

I think we should fly her to Winnipeg.

FRANK Winnipeg?

JUNIOR I don't want these doctors dickin' around with Mom's leg. Christ, we always get the goddamn rejects the cities don't want. *(sarcastic)* "Oh, there's an idiot who can't speak English and can't find work anywhere, let's send him up north." They left a goddamn scalpel in Craig's old lady after her caesarean.

FRANK *(disgusted)* For chrissakes, Junior.

JUNIOR I'm serious. She was complaining about stomach cramps. Stupid bastards thought it was an appendicitis attack. Opened her up and whaddya know? How do you forget a goddamn scalpel in somebody's stomach?! We—

FRANK Jesus, Junior!

JUNIOR We need to get her to Winnipeg, Dad. I'll charter a plane, if I have to. I don't care what it costs.

FRANK I don't know, son. Let's ask your sister what she thinks.

JUNIOR She needs a specialist, Dad. Not a bunch of Jesus freaks.

FRANK Let's see what Mary says.

> *FRANK and JUNIOR stare off in the direction MARY exited.*

> *Lights up on MARY in hospital chapel. She is kneeling in front of an alter, lighting a candle. She makes the sign of the cross and prays.*

> *JUNIOR and FRANK run out of things to say and sit in uncomfortable silence.*

> *BJ sits at his LOIS's bedside.*

MARY Hail Mary, full of grace; the Lord is with thee. Blessed are thou amongst women. And blessed is the fruit of thy womb, Jesus. Holy Mary Mother of God, pray for us sinners now and at the hour of our death. Amen. Hail Mary…

> *Lights come up on BJ. MARY softly prays to herself as BJ speaks.*

BJ   Ma? It's me. BJ. I know you can hear me. You're just pretending to be asleep, right? *(Pause. BJ tries to figure out what all the machines mean. He studies the wires and charts.)* Like the time I went fishin' when I was supposed to be in school. Had my gear stashed under the back porch, ready to make my getaway. Six in the mornin' and I'm tip-toein' around like a mouse on a mission. Even managed to miss all the creaky floorboards! I kept thinkin' you were gonna call out "BJ? Is that you? Where do you think you're going'?" But you just kept quiet. *(He leans in close.)* Like you're doin' now, Ma. But I know you're hearin' everythin'. Right, Ma? *(beat)* I couldn't help pokin' my head in the bedroom to see if you were sleepin.' Whew, I say to myself. I'm home free! Then you open one eye. Real slow. "BillyJoe? How do you think you're gonna catch anything without a net?" I couldn't believe my ears. You actually let me skip school to go in a fishin' derby! *(BJ laughs.)* Come on, Ma. Open your eye like you did that time. *(He takes her hand and holds it.)* Please?

         Lights fade on BJ and come back up on MARY praying.

MARY   …for thine is the kingdom, the power, and the glory, forever and ever. Amen.

         Lights fade on MARY. She gets up, crosses herself at the alter and exits chapel to doctor's office.

         Lights up on JUNIOR and FRANK in waiting room. FRANK thumbs through a travel magazine. He holds up a colourful page of Paris and waves it at JUNIOR.

FRANK   *(tapping page)* See? There. That's right. I'm takin' her to Europe. That's all there is to it.

JUNIOR   Gonna "fly." Eh Dad?

FRANK   She can visit the goddamn Vatican, and lay on a beach in Greece. I'll even hire a bunch of Spics to serenade her under the balcony.

JUNIOR   Better get you some happy pills before you get on a plane.

FRANK   Smart-ass. *(looking around)* Where in the hell is your sister?

JUNIOR	Probably trying to save some poor sick soul from eternal damnation.
FRANK	Be nice, Junior.
JUNIOR	I'm always nice, Pop. In fact, I'm so nice I'm gonna tell you what you should be doing with those RRSPs of yours.
FRANK	Not now, son.

BJ exits LOIS's room and heads for waiting room.

JUNIOR	Diversification is the answer, Dad. High tech, a couple of blue chips.
FRANK	I'll be a mosquito suckin' on a moose's hide arse before I gamble away my life's savings on your say so.
JUNIOR	You want to take her to Europe or not? I'm just saying— I mean if you want to make some extra cash—

BJ enters and interrupts.

FRANK	*(to BJ)* How's your mother?
BJ	Sleepin'.
FRANK	How's she look?
BJ	Like she's sleepin', Dad.
FRANK	*(exasperated)* I need some fresh air. *(to JUNIOR)* You comin'?
JUNIOR	In a minute.

FRANK exits to park bench outside hospital. He walks around, not knowing what to do with himself. He sits on park bench and fidgets.

Dad's takin' her to Europe.

BJ	Yeah, right.
JUNIOR	He's serious this time!
BJ	He hasn't taken her on a holiday in his whole goddamn life. Too afraid to get on a goddamn airplane.
JUNIOR	*(sticks out his hand)* Bet you fifty bucks he does.
BJ	Make it a hundred.

> *BJ goes to shake JUNIOR's hand, JUNIOR pulls his hand away.*

JUNIOR   Not that you ever pay up.

BJ   The only vacation he ever took her on, if you can call it that, was when we drove to the Okanagan.

JUNIOR   *(smiling)* I remember that!

BJ   *(not impressed)* Four kids puking in the car. Some holiday.

JUNIOR   It wasn't that bad.

BJ   *(smiling)* I'll tell you about a good vacation Mom had. When Vicki and I took her to Las Vegas.

JUNIOR   Oh, Christ. Here we go.

BJ   You should have seen her at the slots, Junior. She was lit up like a Christmas tree!

JUNIOR   Yeah, yeah, yeah. And she won a ton of dough. Look Beej, she needs to see a specialist.

> *The actors overlap dialogue, not really listening to what the other one is saying.*

BJ   Jeezus, this one night? I couldn't sleep, eh, so I goes downstairs to the casino to check things out. Anyway, it's like three in the morning…

JUNIOR   This is small-town bullshit. I don't want these idiot doctors near Mom.

BJ   …and when I go down there, guess who's still sittin' at the slot machines? Grinnin' away like a butcher's dog…

JUNIOR   BJ! Enough about Vegas!

BJ   …blisters poppin' outta her hand from pullin' and pullin on the goddamn slots—

JUNIOR   Mom needs to be in a city hospital. She could lose her leg!

> *BJ snaps out of his happy reverie when he hears this. He turns to JUNIOR.*

BJ   *(suddenly angry)* She's not losin' anything! Do you hear me?

> *Beat.*

JUNIOR	*(mellowing)* Okay. I just thought. You know. Winnipeg has some good hospitals, that's all.
BJ	Forget Winnipeg, okay Junior? If it's such a great place why the hell did you move back home?
JUNIOR	*(sarcastic)* Oh, I don't know. Maybe because HBM and S offered me a hundred grand a year to sit around and twiddle my thumbs.
BJ	You gave up a law degree so you could work for a mining company? Makes a lot of sense.
JUNIOR	Hmmm, let's see. *Spend* twenty grand a year going to university or *make* a hundred grand a year to sit around and hire a bunch of miners.
BJ	Right. It had nothin' to do with the fact that in the "big" city you were an eight-ounce perch tryin' to swim around with a bunch of sixty-pound trout.
JUNIOR	Okay, Bush Boy. Whatever you say.
BJ	You know, ever since you came back from Winnipeg, nothing's good enough is it? You don't hunt anymore. You don't fish. What happened to you, anyway?
JUNIOR	Better things to do with my time.
BJ	Like what?
JUNIOR	Play poker with the boys. Have a couple of cold ones.
	JUNIOR raises his flask and drinks. BJ watches him, then stares off. Awkward silence.
	How much did she win, anyway?
BJ	What?
JUNIOR	Mom. How much did she win at the slots?
BJ	I don't know—I'd say about a thousand bucks.
JUNIOR	*(smirking)* Ha! Last time you told this one, Mom only won five hundred.
BJ	*(smiling)* It was really something to see. Really something. *(pause)* I hope he does take her to Europe, you know that?

              (beat, smiling) You should have seen the smile on Mom's face.

JUNIOR   I can go over to the house and see Mom smile for "*free.*"

              MARY enters.

BJ   Any news, Mare?

MARY   *(anxious)* Where's Dad?

JUNIOR   Gettin' some air.

BJ   What'd the doctor say?

MARY   They don't know much more than they did an hour ago.

BJ   Is something wrong?

MARY   No. No. I just want to talk to Dad about a couple of things.

JUNIOR   He said something about Mom having gangrene in her foot.

MARY   What? She doesn't have gangrene.

JUNIOR   That's what Dad said.

BJ   Yeah, well Dad gets a headache and he's got a brain tumour. A little stomach cramp, and it's an appendicitis attack.

MARY   They're not really sure what the problem is.

              MARY starts to exit. FRANK looks at his watch and heads back to the waiting room.

JUNIOR   *(angry)* What do you mean they're not really sure?! They're fuckin' doctors, aren't they? They're supposed to know these things!

              MARY stops.

MARY   Junior. Please. We're in a Catholic hospital.

JUNIOR   Fuckin' rag heads!

BJ   Jesus, Junior. *(to MARY)* I mean, Jeez.

              MARY turns to exit again just as FRANK enters.

MARY   Dad? Can I talk to you for a minute?

FRANK   What's wrong?

MARY *(looking at BJ and JUNIOR)* In private?

FRANK For chrissakes, you heard her.

> *FRANK points with his lips for them to leave. BJ immediately starts to exit. JUNIOR doesn't move.*

JUNIOR I'm not going anywhere.

> *FRANK gives JUNIOR a look. BJ watches this, he stops.*

FRANK *(to MARY)* What? What is it? What's going on?

MARY I don't want you to get excited over nothing because they're not even sure. It's probably just a precautionary thing—they say this stuff, you know.

FRANK What in hell's goin' on?

MARY They said that, well that if the Heparin doesn't work—you know, if they can't thin the blood clot—they may have to — they may have to amputate her leg.

> *When they hear the word "amputate," FRANK, BJ and JUNIOR respond at the same time.*

FRANK Amputate!?

BJ Amputate?

JUNIOR What?

FRANK Whaddya mean amputate? Nobody's amputating anything. I want a goddamn second opinion!

JUNIOR *(pissed off)* That's it! We're sending her to Winnipeg!

MARY Please just calm down. I think they just wanted to prepare us for the worst, you know. So, don't everybody get all excited.

FRANK Jeezus Christ!

JUNIOR She needs to see a specialist!

FRANK She can't lose a leg. It would kill her!

MARY There's a doctor here from Toronto. He's a heart surgeon.

JUNIOR It's her goddamn leg that's screwed, not her heart!

> *Beat.*

BJ   Mare, when will we know?

MARY   In a few days.

JUNIOR   Jeezus Christ.

MARY   We're just going to have to be patient. Have faith. It's
              probably nothing to worry about.

              They all stare at her.

              Everything's going to be okay. You'll see. Mom's going to be
              fine.

              *JUNIOR exits to park bench. He kicks at the dirt, hits the
              bench, then sits and drinks.*

              BJ exits to PAY PHONE.

              FRANK and MARY stay in the waiting room.

              Come on, Dad. Let's see how she's doing.

FRANK   I was thinking maybe you could—you know just—

MARY   —Actually, why don't you wait here. It's probably better if we
              don't crowd her too much.

FRANK   Yeah, yeah. That's a good idea. I'll be out here if you need
              me. You go on now. Go see your mother.

              *MARY exits to LOIS's bedside. She straightens the
              blankets, then washes her LOIS's face. She sits in the chair
              beside her and prays with her rosary beads.*

              *BJ opens an address book and dials. Lights up on JAZ's
              empty apartment. The phone rings and rings. BJ hangs
              up the phone. Lights fade on BJ.*

              *LOIS stirs. MARY is busy checking her IV and doesn't see
              her move.*

              *BJ leaves the pay phone for park bench. FRANK sits in
              waiting room and reads magazines.*

              *Lights up on park bench. JUNIOR is drinking out of
              a flask.*

JUNIOR   *(takes a big swig)* Nobody gives a shit about her but me. She
              could've been in Winnipeg by now.

BJ enters, carrying a canvas bush pack. He sits beside JUNIOR, takes out a piece of wood and a whittling knife from a canvas bag and starts to carve it. JUNIOR watches BJ carve as he drinks.

What are you makin' anyway?

BJ   Nothin'.

Beat.

JUNIOR   You gonna finish this one for a change?

BJ   Maybe.

Beat.

JUNIOR   You making any money on your trapline this year?

BJ   A little.

JUNIOR   You sweat your balls off snowshoeing through the bush in minus forty weather. Costs you money for gas for your skidoo, plus food to survive out there.

BJ   —I eat rabbit stew—doesn't cost anything—

JUNIOR   —you trap a few animals, skin and stretch them. You do all that to earn a "little."

BJ   Yeah.

JUNIOR   I don't know why you never listen to me. I told you. You should take them Yankees out moose hunting or out on your trapline. Do a little guiding. They pay big bucks for that Grizzly Adams shit. You could be makin' a mint.

BJ   I don't want a bunch of people tramping through my trapline.

JUNIOR   You could make some decent cash for once in your life. Invest it in some stocks, for chrissakes.

BJ   Stocks. Right.

BJ shakes his head and laughs.

JUNIOR   You want to work till your eighty, be my guest. I plan on retiring at fifty.

Beat. JUNIOR drinks. BJ continues carving.

BJ	I called Jaz.
JUNIOR	Why?
BJ	Whaddya mean, why? She's her Mom, too.
JUNIOR	She doesn't give a shit.
BJ	Of course she does.
JUNIOR	She didn't come home when Dad had his heart attack.
BJ	She was in Europe.
JUNIOR	I don't care if she was in Timbuk-fuckin'-too. Your Dad has a heart attack, you get your ass home.
BJ	Mom told her not to.
JUNIOR	You and Mom always buy into her bullshit.

BJ carves. JUNIOR watches him.

Well. What did the Weirdo have to say?

BJ	Do you have to call her that?
JUNIOR	No. How about Fucked-up? Or Crazy. Or Flake?

BJ shakes his head.

BJ	Anyway. She wasn't home.
JUNIOR	Lucky for you. Dad would blow a gasket if she showed up.

Beat. JUNIOR watches BJ carve.

Christ, she's dancin' in fuckin' pow wows now. Can you believe that?

BJ	What are you talkin' about?
JUNIOR	I saw a letter she wrote to Mom.
BJ	*(disgusted)* You read Mom's letter?
JUNIOR	It was sittin' there on the coffee table, starin' at me.
BJ	Christ, Junior.
JUNIOR	You're not helping by givin' her your moosehides, you know.
BJ	How did you know about—well, it's better than just throwin' them away.

JUNIOR   She's just gonna use them to dance around *(He pats his hand to his mouth.)* whoo-whoo-whooing all over the place.

        BJ laughs.

        You think that's funny? It's not. It's pathetic. First, it's the punk rockers—safety pins through the ear. Then the hippies—livin' in a house with a bunch of commie wackos. *(pause)* Lesbians, no doubt. Then the breathing heavy "Ooommmm" shit. *(pauses to drink from his flask)* Christ. Why can't she be normal like the rest of us?

BJ   She's searching.

JUNIOR   She needs to search for a fuckin' brain!

        BJ continues to carve.

BJ   C'mon, Junior.

JUNIOR   I'm serious. The wife was talkin' to Lana Ludlow, eh. And Lana's cousin—Ralph—you know, he was married to that fuckin' nutcase, Crazy Mary Bartlet? I think all those bastards are inbred—anyway Lana told Betsy that Crazy Mary is into all that spirit shit—the same stuff as "your" sister. Bunch a witches dancin' around fires, talkin' to dead people, doin' all this voodoo shit.

BJ   Voodoo?

JUNIOR   Lana says Crazy Mary burned down Old Man Marshall's house. Everybody thinks it burnt down on account of him passin' out with a lit cigarette, but Lana says Crazy Mary set it aflame just by lookin' at it. *(pause)* Fuckin' women, eh?

        BJ shakes his head at JUNIOR. JUNIOR drinks. Lights fade on park bench and come up on MARY in LOIS's room. MARY strokes her mother's head.

MARY   You're in God's hands, Mom. *(pause)* Everything's going to be okay. You'll be on your feet in no time. We just need to have faith.

        MARY opens her Bible and reads Psalm 121.

        "I lift up mine eyes to the hills—from where will my help come? My help comes from the Lord, who made heaven and earth. He will not let your foot be moved: he who keeps you will not slumber. He who keeps Israel will neither slumber nor sleep."

> *Mary kisses the Bible and raises it to the heavens. Lights fade on MARY and come up on park bench. JUNIOR offers his flask to BJ. BJ looks at it longingly, then shakes his head no.*

JUNIOR If ever there was a time for whiskey, this would be it. *(waving the flask at him)* Come on, a small one ain't gonna kill ya.

BJ No thanks.

JUNIOR Christ, that AA cult has really brainwashed you hasn't it?

BJ It's not a cult.

JUNIOR Pretty soon you'll be waving crosses in the air—like Saint Mary in there.

BJ It's got nothin' to do with church. And you know, given the circumstances and everything, do you think you could give Mare a break?

JUNIOR I wish she'd give us a break with the Hail Mary's. She's gettin' calluses on her thumb from countin' those fuckin' rosary beads.

BJ Maybe church didn't work for us, but it works for her.

> *JUNIOR laughs.*

JUNIOR Yeah, right.

BJ She helps a lot of people, you know. Visits the elderly, takes care of the sick. She's got a good heart.

JUNIOR Too bad it's filled with guilt. I mean, Jesus, every day she's there praying for our *(mocking priest)* "darkened purgatory souls… oooh, the forsaken ones." Christ.

> *JUNIOR drinks. A beat. He laughs to himself.*

Hey, remember when she used to wear that white tablecloth on her head?

> *BJ and JUNIOR share a laugh.*

BJ She wanted to be a nun so badly, eh?

JUNIOR	She should have. She goes around acting like one, anyway.
BJ	She wanted to have kids.
JUNIOR	Yeah, well that didn't happen did it. Gets married instead of becoming a nun. Then finds out she can't have kids.
BJ	She got a bum rap.
JUNIOR	She could have adopted.
BJ	You know she wanted to. Harry's the one who said no way.
JUNIOR	Well, she should have divorced that loser a long time ago. But, oh no. Divorce would land her in the hot seat for sure. Christ, I tried talkin' to her once about in vitro fertilisation? She almost had a heart attack. "The Good Lord" won't have that. *(JUNIOR mocks voice of the priest and makes the sign of the cross on these four points.)* "Go directly to hell. Do not pass purgatory." Bye bye babies. Bye bye convent.

A long beat. BJ stares at JUNIOR in disbelief. JUNIOR looks over and sees BJ staring at him.

What?

BJ shakes his head at JUNIOR, lost for words.

JUNIOR drinks, then offers the flask to BJ. BJ stares at the bottle, longingly, then carves.

JUNIOR	Hmmm. That's tasty. You sure?
BJ	Not today, thanks.
JUNIOR	Right. One day at a time, eh? I'll drink to that.
BJ	*(getting up)* I'm goin' for a walk.
JUNIOR	C'mon, Beej. I'm just kiddin' ya. I think it's great you're taking a break from the booze. Really. Can't say I miss ya drinkin' my rye. Take a break, then moderate. I'm all for it.
BJ	Yeah. Moderate. Right.
JUNIOR	Well, you're not gonna be like Dad, are you?
BJ	Christ, I hope not.
JUNIOR	I mean, it's not like you're never gonna drink again.

BJ   Just for today, no.

JUNIOR   Right. How long's it been since the old man tied one on?

BJ   Twenty-five years. Although, you'd never know it. He's as dry as the Sahara.

JUNIOR   What's that supposed to mean?

BJ   He's a dry drunk, Junior. He might have put the bottle down, but he still acts like he's drinking. He's still an angry son-of-a-bitch.

JUNIOR   You're not exactly a barrel of laughs yourself.

BJ   I'm just sayin'—there's more to sobriety than just quittin' drinkin'.

JUNIOR   Whaddya talking about? You go to those meetings not to drink, don't ya?

BJ   Yeah and to take a look at why I drank.

JUNIOR   Why? That's easy. You drink to have a good time.

JUNIOR drinks.

BJ   Is that what you're doin'? Havin' a good time?

JUNIOR   You callin' me an alcoholic?

BJ   No.

JUNIOR   I've never lost a job. My kids are well-dressed. We have a nice house. Two cars. A boat. I'm no alcoholic.

BJ   I never said you were. Come on. He's probably wonderin' where we are.

JUNIOR takes another drink.

JUNIOR   *(musically)* "Just for today. Just for today. Keep the booze away. Just for today."

JUNIOR laughs, then gets up unsteadily. JUNIOR picks up BJ's carving and waves it in the air.

Hey, don't forget your chunk of wood!

BJ takes it and helps JUNIOR inside as lights fade. BJ and JUNIOR enter hospital cafeteria and get a coffee.

Lights up on LOIS's bedside. There's an extreme beep on the heart monitor. MARY jumps. Beeping returns to normal. MARY exits to doctor's office.

Lights up on waiting room. FRANK is asleep on the couch, a travel magazine in his lap. The sound of whispering Northern Lights, Native drumming, rattles and chanting wakes him up. FRANK looks around, gives his head a shake and rubs his ears. Chanting fades. He flips through the travel magazine.

MARY returns to LOIS's room.

JAZ enters. She wears her hair in braids and is dressed in jeans and a fringed hide, beaded jacket. She wears a medicine pouch around her neck and carries her Native-looking duffel bag. She stands and watches FRANK. Finally, she enters. This is the first time she's seen or spoken to him in ten years.

JAZ   Hi, Dad.

FRANK looks up at JAZ. He stares at her, then resumes reading his magazine.

Beat.

JUNIOR and BJ enter. JUNIOR sees her first.

JUNIOR   Well, if it isn't Poco-fuckin-hontas!

BJ   *(surprised)* Jaz?

JAZ   Hey, Beej.

BJ goes to JAZ, picks her up and gives her a big hug.

BJ   *(to JAZ)* Hey, it's good to see you. How did you know about—I mean—

JUNIOR   *(to BJ)* Liar.

JUNIOR gives BJ a look. BJ shrugs as in "I didn't tell her."

JAZ stares at FRANK.

JAZ   *(to FRANK)* How's Mom?

JUNIOR   How should she be? We're in a hospital. What's in the bag?

JAZ	Just some of my things. *(to FRANK)* How... how're you making out, Dad?
	FRANK doesn't respond.
BJ	*(gently)* Want some coffee, Little? A sandwich, maybe? The food's pretty good here. For hospital food, anyway.
JUNIOR	Looks like an Injun bag to me.
BJ	*(to JUNIOR)* Give it a rest, will ya?
JAZ	*(to FRANK)* I got here as fast as I could, Dad.
JUNIOR	*(to BJ)* You've got a big mouth, Beej.
BJ	I didn't—It's her mother too, for chrissake!
FRANK	Watch your language, boy. We're in a goddamn Catholic hospital, eh.
	BJ and JUNIOR laugh.
	What's so goddamn funny?
BJ	Nothin', Dad.
JAZ	Where is she?
	BJ nods his head. JAZ starts to head for curtained room.
BJ	In there, Mary's with her right now. We're just going in one at a time.
	JAZ stops.
JAZ	How long do you think she'll be?
BJ	I don't know.
JAZ	Maybe I could just peek my head in?
JUNIOR	Didn't you hear BJ? We're only going in one at a time.
BJ	I'm sure she'll be out soon. Did you fly?
JAZ	Yeah.
BJ	Flight okay?
JAZ	Yeah.
BJ	That's good.

Awkward silence.

Soooo. *(beat)* Hey, you want to grab a coffee, Little?

JAZ I'd like to see Mom first.

    MARY exits LOIS's room and enters waiting room, looking very tired.

Hi, Mare.

MARY *(startled)* What—what are you—how did you—?

    JAZ hugs her. MARY, shocked to see JAZ, doesn't reciprocate the hug.

JAZ I'm doing great, thanks. I got on the soonest plane I could.

    MARY gives BJ a look. BJ shrugs again. MARY walks over to a chair and sits. JAZ follows her.

How's Mom?

MARY She's holding her own.

JAZ Can I see her?

MARY Not right now. The doctors are in there.

JAZ How… how long will they be?

MARY I don't know. A while.

JAZ Is she… is she in a lot of pain?

MARY No. They've got her on a morphine drip.

JAZ Morphine?

MARY *(sadly)* She's not conscious.

JAZ *(tears welling)* She's not conscious?

BJ But, she can hear, right Mare? *(to JAZ)* You know Ma, Little. Nothin' ever gets by her.

MARY *(to JAZ)* You're going to have to pull yourself together, Jaz. The last thing Mom needs is for you to have a breakdown.

JUNIOR Yeah. Mom doesn't need to be worrying about you right now. She needs her strength.

> *JAZ tries to collect herself. Beat. JAZ stares off toward LOIS's room. MARY inspects JAZ.*

MARY   Your hair's long.

JAZ   Yeah.

MARY   That the style in the city?

JAZ   It's just easy.

MARY   It certainly is different.

JUNIOR   Need money for a hair cut?

> *JUNIOR pulls out some change from his pocket and shakes it in front of JAZ. He laughs.*

BJ   I like it.

JUNIOR   It's too injun-looking, if you ask me.

BJ   *(to JUNIOR)* No one asked you.

FRANK   *(to MARY)* What are they doin' to her?

MARY   Checking her vitals. I'll see how much longer they're going to be.

> *MARY starts to exit. JAZ follows.*

JAZ   I'll come with you.

FRANK   *(still looking at magazine)* Let your sister handle it.

MARY   It'd be better if you wait here. I'll be right back.

> *MARY exits to LOIS's room. A bewildered JAZ stares after her. Awkward silence.*

JUNIOR   How'd you afford a flight home?

BJ   She sold a couple of her paintings—didn't you Jaz?

JAZ   What?

BJ   Mom said you sold some paintings?

JAZ   *(still looking toward LOIS's room)* Yeah.

JUNIOR   How much you make?

JAZ   I did all right.

JUNIOR	How much is all right?
	Beat. JAZ stares off toward LOIS's room.
	Hello?!
JAZ	A thousand dollars. I made a thousand dollars, okay?
JUNIOR	A piece?
JAZ	For both. *(to BJ)* Beej, has Mom been—
JUNIOR	How many hours do you spend on a painting?
JAZ	What?
JUNIOR	How long does it take you to do a painting?
JAZ	It depends.
JUNIOR	On what?
JAZ	It just depends, Junior. I don't time it. *(to BJ)* Has she been on morphine since she got here, Beej?
BJ	Pretty much.
JUNIOR	Well, how much do you make an hour?
JAZ	I don't know Junior. It doesn't work like that.
JUNIOR	It works exactly like that. You calculate how many hours you put in and then take the total of what you made and divide it by the hours. And that's how much you make an hour.
BJ	Anybody hungry?
JUNIOR	Not that difficult to figure out.
JAZ	It's not about the money, Junior.
JUNIOR	Right. You'd rather be a starving artist.
JAZ	What. Ever. Junior.
BJ	You should probably eat something, Dad. You know, your blood sugar and all. Come on *Junior*, let's go get some food.
FRANK	You go. I need to talk to Junior about something.
BJ	Oh. *(pause)* Okay. Come on, Little.
JAZ	Think I'll just wait here. I'd like to see Mom first.

JUNIOR	She's not going anywhere.

> *JUNIOR snaps his fingers at JAZ and points toward the cafeteria as in "get lost." Exasperated, JAZ quickly gets up and walks away. BJ follows after her.*

BJ	They got great milkshakes in this place, Little. Remember the time you tried to make your own?...

> *BJ puts his arm around a reluctant JAZ and leads her off stage. She looks over her shoulder, toward LOIS's room.*

...Christ, that was funny. You forgot to put the lid on the blender. Man, there was chocolate everywhere...

> *As FRANK and JUNIOR talk in the waiting room, JAZ and BJ enter cafeteria. BJ picks up a tray of food from the counter—two hamburgers, fries, a coke and a milkshake. JAZ sits at a table, and nervously rearranges the salt and pepper shakers. BJ joins her.*

FRANK	*(firmly)* I want you to book me a couple of tickets to Paris. Now.

> *FRANK gets up and thrusts the travel magazine at JUNIOR.*

JUNIOR	But, Dad—
FRANK	I am taking her to Europe.
JUNIOR	Don't you think you should wait until—
FRANK	Never mind, I'll do it myself.

> *FRANK tries to grab the magazine back. JUNIOR pulls it away.*

JUNIOR	Okay. Okay. When do you want to go?
FRANK	On her birthday. And I want you to book us in the fanciest goddamn hotel you can find. And they'd better speak English, too!
JUNIOR	All right, Dad. You got it.

> *JUNIOR starts to exit.*

FRANK	And son?

JUNIOR   What?

FRANK   *(pointing with his lips at the cup in JUNIOR's hand)* Is that just coffee you're drinkin' there?

JUNIOR   Of course, it's just coffee, Dad.

FRANK   If I recall correctly, meetings are Tuesdays and Thursdays.

JUNIOR   Yeah, yeah.

> *JUNIOR staggers slightly as he exits to park bench. FRANK watches him go, then picks up BJ's carving and inspects it. He tosses the carving back on the waiting room couch. JUNIOR drinks from a flask. Lights fade on park bench and waiting room.*
>
> *Lights come up on hospital cafeteria. BJ sip a coke and a milkshake and eats a couple of burgers.*

BJ   I tried callin' you.

JAZ   Yeah?

BJ   Didn't want to leave a message—you know—didn't want you to worry. But, doesn't matter cause you made it anyway. That's kinda weird, eh?

JAZ   I guess. How's Mom?

BJ   She's holdin' her own. Mare says the doctors have everything under control.

JAZ   What happened?

BJ   Got a blood clot in her leg.

JAZ   A blood clot?

BJ   She's going to be okay. That Heparin stuff is supposed to loosen it up.

JAZ   What Heparin stuff?

BJ   It's some kind of blood thinner. You know Ma, Little. She'll be up and around in no time.

> *JAZ takes this in.*

So, how's life in Vancouver, anyway?

JAZ	Pretty good.
BJ	Maybe I'll come out there and visit you one day?
JAZ	That'd be great, Beej.
BJ	Hear there's lots of geese in that big park you got out there.
	BJ pretends to shoot a rifle in the air, complete with sound effects.
JAZ	Beej!
BJ	Show those city slickers how real men live, eh? Send a few guccis tappin' down the street.
	JAZ laughs. BJ makes goose calls.
JAZ	*(pointing to a leather sheath on his belt)* You'd have to leave your knife at home, Grizzly Adams.
BJ	Are you kiddin'? All those murderers out there?
JAZ	It's not like that, Beej.
BJ	Hey, I watch the news, you know? Those city kids are knifin' each other over a leather jacket.
JAZ	I live in Kitsilano. Right by the beach. It's safe.
BJ	You ever miss it here?
JAZ	I miss you.
BJ	I mean, the bush? The lakes?
JAZ	Yeah. Yeah, sure I do.
BJ	Personally, this town's gettin' too big for me.
JAZ	*(facetious)* Yeah, I noticed the sign on the road. "Flin Flon. Home of Bobby Clarke. Population: Six thousand." *(She chuckles.)*
BJ	Fifty-nine hundred too many for me. Thinkin' about movin' to the "Chalet" full time.
JAZ	What "chalet"?
BJ	My trapper's cabin.
	JAZ laughs.

Don't laugh. She's a beaut. Cut and peeled the logs myself. Floor to ceiling windows. Nice little wood stove. And lots of peace and quiet.

JAZ   *(sarcastic)* I'm sure Vicki and the girls would love that.

BJ   Actually, Roberta wouldn't mind livin' out there. Trapped her first animal this year.

JAZ   Really? That's great.

BJ   Yeah. Except for the fact that now when anybody drops by for a visit, she starts yellin'; "Hey, wanna see my beaver?! Wanna see my beaver?!"

> *JAZ laughs.*

Have to admit, she's pretty good. I mean, she's only ten. Reminds me a lot of you when you were a kid. Man, you could set a rabbit snare, Little. Fastest hands in the north, eh? *(He moves his hands around in lightening speed, recalling JAZ's rabbit snare prowess, complete with sound effects.)*

JAZ   *(smiling)* Guess I had a good teacher.

BJ   What can I say? Hey, we'll haveta get you out on the trapline while you're home.

JAZ   Yeah. I'd like that. Hey, Beej, I—

> *BJ cuts her off. He drifts into reveries of his trapper's cabin. JAZ is more concerned with how to bring up the fact that the wants to use the medicines on her mother. She tries to interject, but to no avail.*

BJ   *(smiling)* —You should see the view from there, Little. Nothin' but trees and lake—

JAZ   Beej, I want to—

BJ   —took me two trips to get those goddamn windows out there, eh? Had them wrapped in—

JAZ   Listen, Beej. I—

BJ   —in sleeping bags in the back of my truck. I drive—like I'm goin' to a funeral, avoidin' all the potholes and everything. Take them out of the sleepin' bags real slow and carefully

	balance them on my canoe. My new canoe, I might add. Built her last year. A sixteen-footer. Cedar for days.
JAZ	There's something I want to—
BJ	Anyway… so I'm glidin' over the water with these windows hangin' over the sides. Then I haveta hoof them onto my back and carry them over not one, but three, goddamn portages. By the time I get to the Chalet I'm so goddamn tired that I got no steam left in me to put the windows in, eh. I figure I'll come back and do it the next weekend. So, I leave them leanin' there against the Chalet, glimmerin' in the sunlight. When I come back, whaddya think I see?
JAZ	I don't know.
BJ	Goddamn broken glass everywhere.
JAZ	What happened?
BJ	Bloody bear has busted them to bits. Couldn't believe my goddamn eyes.
JAZ	Ooh, that hurts.
BJ	Not really. *(big smile fills his face)* Cause now I got me a big, ol' bear skin rug layin' right in front of the woodstove.
JAZ	Beej, you didn't!
BJ	I had to. Coulda eaten one of my kids.
	Beat.
JAZ	What did you do with the claws?
BJ	Whaddya mean, what did I do with them? Last time I looked they were still attached to the bear. Why?
	A beat.
JAZ	I was just wondering.
BJ	You want one? I'll clip one off for you.
JAZ	Yeah. Bear medicine is very powerful.
BJ	Tell me about it. Those windows were an inch thick!
JAZ	Bear is the healer. He teaches us to go within ourselves and face our fears. Kind of like going into the cave to hibernate.

BJ	Whatever you say, Tonto.

Lights fade on BJ and JAZ in cafeteria and come up on JUNIOR at park bench. He has the travel magazine opened and is on his cell phone, talking to his wife.

JUNIOR   *(irritated)* Make sure the hotel staff speak English, too. On her birthday. *(pause, more irritated)* I know it's just a month away. You don't think I know when my own mother's birthday is? *(pause)* Look, I'll do it myself. *(pause)* Just put it on the visa. And call me at the hospital to confirm. Where's Sarah? *(pause, more agitated)* Well, put her on. *(pause, sweetly)* Hi, baby. *(pause)* How's Daddy's angel? *(pause)* Yeah, Grandma's kinda sick. *(pause)* She's got a sore leg. *(pause)* Not tonight, baby. Grandma's sleeping. Maybe you can see her tomorrow. *(pause)* No, I can't tonight honey. Mommy will have to take you. *(pause)* You can show me all your new ballet moves tomorrow, okay? *(pause)* Okay, baby. Daddy's got to go. *(pause)* I love you, too. *(in a baby voice)* Bye. Bye.

JUNIOR stares at the phone. He drinks from his flask.

Cafeteria. Lights up on JAZ and BJ.

JAZ   Why is everybody so ashamed of being Indian?

BJ   Whaddya mean?

JAZ   Nobody talks about it. Nobody even admits it.

BJ   Well, we're about a hundredth—if that. Dad's great-great grandmother was a half-breed or somethin'. That makes us practically nothin'.

JAZ   You know a few years ago when Mom came out on one of her visits? She told me a few things. You know, to try to help me understand Dad a little better. Anyway, I was sworn to secrecy so I'm not supposed to say anything.

BJ   I'm all ears.

JAZ   Mom told me that Dad's mom—our grandmother—was a full-blood Cree Indian.

BJ   Get outta here.

JAZ   Dad spent the first ten years of his life on a reserve just outside of Saskatoon.

BJ	Mom told you that?
JAZ	It's true. I swear.
BJ	Dad's a half-breed?
JAZ	Métis.
BJ	*(shocked)* Well, I'll be goddamned.
JAZ	*(smiling)* Why do you think he always points at everything with his lips? *(pointing in several directions with her lips)*
BJ	What?
JAZ	Never mind. Anyway. Grandma died when Dad was in his early twenties. Mom actually met her once.
BJ	Jeezuz Christ.
JAZ	Beej. The past ten years I've.... Well, I've been learning about our culture. From the Elders. The teachings are beautiful.
BJ	I'm happy for you, Little. Really. But—just because— I mean—even if Dad "is" a half-breed—
JAZ	We're Métis.
BJ	Well. It means nothin' to me. We were raised white.
JAZ	We weren't raised white. How many people do you know who trap, hunt and fish year-round?
BJ	Trappin' ain't an Indian thing. It's a northern thing.
JAZ	Beej, there are six thousand people in this town and you're the only one I know who traps. Other than Harold Bear— and he's a full-blood Cree.
BJ	Look, Little just because—
JAZ	I've done a lot of healing in the Sweat Lodge, Beej. This one Medicine Woman, "Running Buffalo"—has been teaching me about the sacred medicines. I… I've talked with our ancestors, Beej. They come to me all the time, now. One time they hurled me right out of my bed in the middle of the night. I ended up right on my butt. They said I wasn't payin' attention. That I needed to listen to what they were tellin' me.

BJ looks at her incredulously.

BJ   (*joking*) So, whaddya sayin'? This Buffalo Woman threw you out of your bed?

   Beat.

JAZ   Okay. I know this is going to sound a bit out there, but I didn't just "happen" to come home for a visit. Mom came to me. She was lying in a hospital bed. (*pause*) She… (*JAZ holds her hands out like her mother did in the vision, beckoning her home.*) …Beej, she called me home.

   Beat. BJ continues to stare at JAZ.

   Lights fade on cafeteria and come up on waiting room.

   MARY exits from LOIS's room to waiting room where FRANK is sleeping. She watches him, then gently taps him on the shoulder. FRANK jumps.

MARY   You want to lay down in Junior's van, Dad?

FRANK   (*coming to*) What for? I'm not sleepy.

MARY   Okay. (*pause*) You want something from the cafeteria?

   FRANK sits up.

FRANK   Nah.

MARY   You're gonna have to eat something, Dad. We don't want you getting sick, too.

FRANK   I can't even think about food right now. (*stands*) I'm going to talk to that bloody doctor.

   FRANK starts to exit to doctor's office in his sock feet. MARY picks up his shoes and follows after him. She taps him on the shoulder. He turns. She hands him his shoes. He continues offstage. MARY watches him go, then exits to LOIS's room.

   Lights fade on waiting room and come up on cafeteria.

BJ   Look, Little. I'm glad you're finding peace, but—

JAZ   I want to use the medicines on Mom.

BJ   What?

JAZ	I want to do a cleansing ceremony with her.
BJ	The nurses are giving her sponge baths.
JAZ	I'm talking about smudging her.
BJ	Smudg—ing?
JAZ	It's a purification ceremony. A spiritual ceremony. You light sage and sweetgrass in a bowl and carry the smoke over your body.
BJ	Smoke.
JAZ	It gets rid of negative energies.
BJ	*(looking around)* Negative energies? Come on, Jaz.
JAZ	I really thought, you of all people, would understand.
BJ	Nobody's gonna let you burn anything in a hospital. I can't even smoke in here.
JAZ	It's important, Beej.
BJ	What are you going to say? Guess what everybody? We're Indian! Now, if you'll excuse me, I want to do a little voodoo here.
JAZ	It's not voodoo.
BJ	They won't go for it.
JAZ	Please talk to them, Beej.
BJ	Me?
JAZ	They'll listen to you.
BJ	Yeah, right. You know what Junior's reaction will be. Mary would throw an absolute fit. And Dad? Jesus Christ.
JAZ	What about you?
BJ	What about me?
JAZ	AA's based on spiritual principals, isn't it?
BJ	Yeah. So?
JAZ	Well, do you believe in the Creator?
BJ	I believe there's something out there. What, I'm not sure.

JAZ	It's all the same spirit, Beej.
BJ	Maybe.

> *Lights fade on cafeteria and come up on MARY, praying at LOIS's bedside. She clutches her rosary beads.*

MARY	Father, please help me. I don't know if I can keep it together. I was fine until I saw Jaz. It made me remember when we were little—and Mom was playing hopscotch with her. Oh, God. I don't know what I'll do if she loses her leg. Please, Lord. Give me strength. Give me the faith I need to get through this. Amen. *(pause)* "I believe in one God, the Father Almighty, Creator of heaven and earth. I believe in Jesus Christ, his only son our Lord… "

> *Lights fade on MARY and come up on cafeteria. BJ sits. JAZ is standing behind him, her arms lovingly draped around his neck.*

JAZ	Look, I just want a few minutes with her. Just to smudge her. Say a few prayers. Sing a few songs.
BJ	They won't go for it.
JAZ	I'm talking about a ten-minute ceremony.
BJ	Come on, Little. You can't have stuff smokin' in a hospital.

> *JAZ stops hugging him.*

JAZ	Maybe we could just wheel her bed outside or something.
BJ	You have got to be kidding.
JAZ	She needs the medicines, Beej.
BJ	You really think you can make Mom's leg better by smoking stuff and singing some songs?
JAZ	The songs call the ancestors from the Spirit World. They're the ones who have the power to heal.
BJ	What are you sayin'? Dead people are going to come down and heal Mom? What if they throw *her* out of bed? Come on, Jaz.

JAZ   It's not like that. It's… it's hard to explain. The medicines are very powerful, Beej. *(clutching her Native bag)* I've seen them work miracles.

BJ   Okay. You know what? This is like waaay out there for me. I mean, dead people. Smoke? Smudg-ing? It's… it's uh…. Look, why don't you just say some prayers when you're in there with her.

        A beat as JAZ thinks about it. JUNIOR staggers from park bench to cafeteria.

JAZ   *(sighing)* Okay. Okay. But, will you at least keep Mary preoccupied so I can be alone with Mom?

BJ   You're not thinkin' about smokin' up her room are you?

JAZ   No.

BJ   Promise?

JAZ   I promise. I just want to sing some songs.

BJ   Sing some songs. That's it?

JAZ   And drum. *(pause)* Quietly.

        BJ considers her proposal.

BJ   Okay.

JAZ   Thanks Beej.

        JAZ gives him a big hug. JUNIOR staggers in and witnesses this. He's had "a few." He puts one arm around BJ and one around JAZ.

JUNIOR   *(slurring)* Whadda we got here? A little family bonding?

        He laughs, pours himself a glass of water, picks up a plate of burger and fries from the cafeteria and plops himself down on a chair.

        MARY crosses herself and leaves LOIS's room for cafeteria.

        (looking around) Hey, where's Saint Mary? I'm sure she wouldn't want to miss out on this "pow wow," eh Jaz?

> *JUNIOR takes a bite of his burger and dramatically spits it out.*

(spitting food out) Fuck. There's ketchup on here!

BJ   Scrape it off.

JUNIOR   It's soaked into the bun.

JAZ   Here, have mine.

> *JAZ pushes her plate toward him. MARY enters cafeteria. JUNIOR pushes it back.*

JUNIOR   I ain't eatin' no plant burger!

JAZ   *(to MARY)* Can I see her now?

MARY   Maybe give them a few more minutes.

> *MARY pours herself some water.*

BJ   Take my bun, for chrissakes.

> *BJ tries to hand JUNIOR his uneaten burger.*

JUNIOR   You got onions on yours.

BJ   Pretend they're dollar bills.

JUNIOR   Aren't you just a laugh a fucking minute.

BJ   *(to MARY)* Any news, Mare?

MARY   Dad's in with the doctor right now.

JUNIOR   You want my burger?

> *JUNIOR unsteadily tries to hand MARY his burger and knocks into the table, sending the drinks and food flying onto the floor. MARY cleans up the mess.*

Let the goddamn Pakis pick it up!

MARY   Junior LaFontaine!

JAZ   Why are you so racist?

JUNIOR   Fuck you!

BJ   Chill out, Junior.

JUNIOR   No!

JUNIOR purposely picks up another cup and drops it on the floor.

MARY looks around, embarrassed.

MARY   (*whispering*) Junior. Pull. Yourself. Together.

MARY continues to clean up the mess.

JAZ picks up her bag. She nods to BJ, then starts to exit.

JUNIOR   (*calling after JAZ*) Where you goin'?

JAZ   To see Mom.

JUNIOR   You don't give a shit about Mom!

JAZ keeps walking.

BJ   Junior, knock it off.

JAZ exits to LOIS's room.

JUNIOR   (*yelling after her*) You haven't been home in ten years! Ten fuckin' years!

MARY   Junior, please. People are staring.

JUNIOR   Fuck 'em. I don't care.

JUNIOR looks toward the audience. He walks toward them.

What?! What are you lookin' at? My mother's about to have her fuckin' leg hacked off, okay? Okay?!

MARY picks up the pieces of the broken cup. BJ puts his arm around JUNIOR and leads him out of cafeteria to waiting room.

BJ   We don't know that for sure. Come on, buddy. It's going to be okay.

JUNIOR   No, it's not! What's Mom gonna do with one leg?

BJ and JUNIOR exit to waiting room.

MARY   (*to herself*) We're going to be okay. It's going to be okay. It's going to be okay. Everything's going to be okay.

Lights fade on cafeteria as MARY neatly piles the plates, cups and napkin dispenser back on the table.

Lights up on LOIS's room. JAZ is checking out the machines, running the tubes through her fingers. She fights back tears. JAZ sits beside her mother and strokes her hair.

JAZ   It's good to see you, Mom. *(pause)* It's good to be home. I don't have long. The nurses will be in soon. I'm going to do a cleansing ceremony, Mom. Remember when you were in Vancouver and we smudged? Sort of like that without the smoke.

JAZ places her Native bag on the bedside table. She takes out a drum and drum stick, a cloth-covered feather holder, a string of prayer ties—red, yellow, black and white, blue and green (they look like pouches), a healing rattle. She hangs the prayer ties from the IV unit.

Lights fade on JAZ as she prepares for ceremony.

Lights come up on FRANK. FRANK exits doctor's office and leans against the door. Beat. He heads for the waiting room.

MARY exits cafeteria. She sees FRANK walking toward the waiting room. He is obviously upset. She follows after him.

MARY   Dad?

He continues walking. She catches up to him in the waiting room.

FRANK   They're gonna do it. They're gonna cut off her leg.

They all sink into silence. Lights fade.

Lights up on JAZ. She lightly drums and sings a healing song in Cree: "Muskwa omanitouma" ("Bear Spirit" translation on page 101).

JAZ   Muskwa, Muskwa
       kiya ki-maskawsin
       Muskwa, Muskwa
       nikamo nanatawih nikamowin
       astum maskihkiy muskwa
       nanatawiha maskihna
       astum maskihkiy muskwa

omanitoma masiskeweat
Hey ya Hey yo

> *Lights up on waiting room. As JAZ sings, FRANK watches BJ carve.*

FRANK   *(to BJ)* If you're gonna be doin' that in here, make sure you clean up those goddamn wood chips, eh?

BJ   I will.

> *Frank scoops BJ's ballcap off his head and puts it on the seat.*

FRANK   Your mother isn't gonna bloody well do it for you now, you know.

> *BJ doesn't respond.*

JUNIOR   *(to FRANK)* Christ, what's takin' them so long?

FRANK   They're waiting for an operating room. That doctor said he'd come get us as soon as they know anything.

JUNIOR   There's only one friggin' operating room in this hospital?

FRANK   Don't you start in about Winnipeg.

> *Lights fade on waiting room and come up on JAZ. She continues to sing in Cree.*

JAZ   Muskwa, Muskwa
Kiya ki – maskwasin…

> *Lights fade on JAZ and come up on waiting room.*

> *MARY starts to exit to LOIS's room.*

BJ   Where you goin', Mare?

MARY   To check on Mom.

BJ   Uh… Jaz is still with her.

MARY   She's been in there long enough.

> *MARY starts to exit again. BJ jumps up.*

BJ   Hey, Mare?

> *MARY stops.*

MARY   Yeah.

BJ   Can I talk to you a minute?

MARY   What?

> *BJ doesn't know what to say. He motions for her to join him off to the side—in private. They move a few steps away from FRANK and JUNIOR. MARY stares at him, concerned. He holds up his carving.*

BJ   Uh… do you think this should be a fox or a bear?

MARY   *(dumbfounded)* BJ, can this wait?

> *BJ shrugs. MARY starts to exit to LOIS's room.*
>
> *JAZ drums and sings louder.*

JAZ   …muskwa, muskwa
            nikamo nanatawih nikamowin
            astum maskihkiy muskwa
            nanatawiha maskihna…

> *BJ throws a coughing fit to cover up JAZ's drumming. MARY stops.*

MARY   *(to BJ)* Beej, are you okay? I'll get you some water.

> *MARY gets him a glass of water from the water cooler, situated a few feet away.*

FRANK   Christ, maybe it's time to give up smoking.

BJ   *(still choking)* Yep. Yep.

> *MARY comes back with water. BJ continues to cough. He drinks the water and slowly recovers.*
>
> *MARY start to exit toward LOIS's room. BJ jumps up.*

            Mare, I'll come with you.

> *MARY stops.*

MARY   It's okay.

> *Lights up on JAZ. She takes an eagle feather out of its holder and brushes the feather over her mother's body. She sings in Cree.*

JAZ   …astum maskihkiy muskwa
             Omanitou masiskeweat
             Hey ya Hey yo.

             *When she finishes with the feather, JAZ picks up the
             healing rattle and shakes it over her mother—from head
             to toe.*

             *BJ hears the rattle and chanting, grabs his stomach and
             doubles over.*

BJ   Ohhhh.

FRANK   Christ, what's wrong with you now?

MARY   Beej, what is it?

BJ   *(moaning)* Ohhhhh. My stomach. Ooooh.

MARY   Come here. Sit down.

             MARY helps him to a chair in the waiting room.

BJ   *(still moaning)* Oooh.

JUNIOR   *(to BJ)* Jee-zuz Christ.

             *JAZ stops chanting and shaking the rattle. She raises both
             of her hands in Native prayer (palms toward her and
             upward to the sky).*

MARY   *(to BJ)* I'll get a nurse.

BJ   *(suddenly)* No! *(sitting up)* I… I think I'll be okay. Probably
             just indigestion.

JAZ   *Ninieskomon ni manitou. Ayayawes niwakomakunak.*

             JAZ packs up her medicines.

MARY   You sure you're okay?

             *BJ takes MARY's hand and tries to nonchalantly look at
             her watch—more obvious, than nonchalant. Ten minutes
             is up.*

BJ   *(recovering)* Yeah. Whew.

             MARY stares at him.

JUNIOR   Told ya you shouldn't have eaten all those onions.

BJ   Stomach's not used to all the chemicals they put in store-bought meat.

FRANK   You might want to think about varying your moose diet, boy. You're gonna start growin' antlers soon.

> *FRANK laughs at his own joke. JUNIOR joins in. MARY heads for LOIS's room. JAZ exits LOIS's room and heads for waiting room. MARY and JAZ almost bump into each other.*

MARY   *(quietly to JAZ)* They're going to do it. They're going to amputate Mom's leg.

> *JAZ takes this in. She is obviously upset. MARY softens. Instead of going into LOIS's room, she follows after JAZ. She awkwardly places her hand on JAZ's back, then moves away.*

JUNIOR   *(to JAZ)* Christ, you were in there long enough. What were you doin'?

> *JAZ doesn't respond. She takes in the amputation news. BJ changes the subject.*

BJ   You know, I've been thinking. We could use the old deck wood for a ramp. Put it right outside by the rose garden, Dad.

JUNIOR   That's stupid. It needs to be by the front door.

BJ   If we borrowed Mr. Zelski's backhoe, we could dig up those big rocks and have the whole thing built by next week.

FRANK   That old fart? He's so cheap he squeezes a nickel until the beaver shits.

> *BJ and JUNIOR laugh. MARY looks at her dad and shakes her head.*

MARY   *(mildly disgusted)* Honestly, Dad. Where do you get these sayings, anyway?

FRANK   Well, it's true.

> *Suddenly, a loud beeping noise is heard from inside LOIS's room. They all stare.*

What the hell is that?!

MARY	Get the doctor!

MARY rushes for LOIS's room. JAZ follows her.

JUNIOR	Jesus Christ!
MARY	*(over her shoulder)* Hurry! Hurry!

BJ rushes to get the doctor. FRANK and JUNIOR stand there, paralysed.

Cross-fade. Lights fade on FRANK and JUNIOR and soft spot comes up on LOIS's bed. It is empty.

Soft spot on FRANK. He hears the same Native drumming, chanting and whispering Northern Lights. He looks around the room, over his shoulders—trying to figure out where the sound is coming from. He rubs his ears, gives his head a shake. Whispering Northern Lights, chanting and drumming stops. (Note: Sound effects end with four drum-beats that sound like a heartbeat. (i.e., Boom-boom. Boom-boom. Boom-boom. Boom-boom.)

Full lights up on waiting room.

The mood is ominous. FRANK stares into space. JUNIOR vaguely reads a newspaper. BJ sort of carves. JAZ sort of sketches. MARY paces, slowly, rosary beads in hand.

JUNIOR throws the newspaper down and gets up. He is angry.

JUNIOR	For chrissakes! When are we going to know something?
JAZ	The nurse said it shouldn't be too much longer.
JUNIOR	They've been sayin' that for five fuckin' hours!
BJ	These things take time, Junior.
MARY	I'll go see what's taking so long.

MARY exits to doctor's office.

JUNIOR	We should've sent her to Winnipeg. Mom wouldn't be in there right now if she'd had decent doctors looking after her!
BJ	Nobody could've predicted this, Junior.

JUNIOR   She had fuckin' water around her heart! How did they miss that?

    JUNIOR storms off to cafeteria. He drinks from his flask.

FRANK   *(staring after JUNIOR)* That kid's just like me. Can't stand to see his mother in pain.

    BJ stops carving. He attempts to say something then changes his mind.

Remember the time your mother slipped on that ice on the sidewalk and twisted her ankle? Junior must have been about seven. Maybe eight. Anyway, you'd think she'd broken her leg in five places the way he carried on. She couldn't even blow her goddamn nose on her own. Junior was right in there with the Kleenex tellin' her to blow.

    BJ looks over at FRANK.

BJ   Actually, that was me, Dad.

FRANK   No, it wasn't. You don't think I know my own goddamn kids?

    BJ carves furiously. Lights fade.

    Soft spot comes up on JAZ in waiting room. She hears the same Native drumming, chanting and whispering Northern Lights as FRANK. She stares at the empty bed, suspiciously. Whispering Northern Lights, drumming and chanting fades with four heartbeat rhythm drum beats.

    Soft spot remains on JAZ and fades slowly.

    Lights come back up on waiting room. MARY exits doctor's office. She is obviously shaken. She takes out a Kleenex and wipes her eyes and nose. She crosses herself and heads for waiting room.

    BJ continues to carve. JAZ sketches. FRANK looks through the travel magazine.

    A teary MARY passes JUNIOR just outside the waiting room.

JUNIOR   *(to MARY)* What the hell's goin' on?

    MARY keeps walking.

Mare!

> *MARY enters waiting room. JUNIOR follows her in. She stares at her family. She takes a deep breath, trying to regain her composure. JAZ sees her first.*

JAZ   Mare?

> *FRANK opens his eyes. Everybody stops doing what they're doing and looks at her. MARY starts to cry. FRANK jumps up.*

FRANK   What is it?

MARY   *(shaky)* It's Mom.

FRANK   What's wrong?

MARY   She… she—

> *MARY breaks into tears.*

FRANK   Is it her leg? What?

MARY   She… has… cancer.

FRANK   Ca-cancer?

> *JAZ, BJ, JUNIOR respond at the same time.*

JAZ   No. No.

BJ   Oh, God. Oh, my God.

JUNIOR   I want a second opinion!

BJ   She was fine. Three days ago, she was fine.

FRANK   Can't they do something? Amputate?

> *MARY shakes her head, no.*

MARY   *(through tears)* It's not just her leg… it's everywhere. It's everywhere!

> *JAZ breaks into tears. BJ tries to comfort her.*

JUNIOR   We're getting her to Winnipeg. They'll be able to do something. Operate. Chemotherapy. There are things they can do!

FRANK   *(loud and angry)* Where's that doctor?! I want to talk to the goddamn doctor! NOW!

> *FRANK storms offstage.*
>
> *Blackout.*
>
> *The sound of whispering Northern Lights, drumming and chanting in the dark.*
>
> *End of Act One.*

Act Two

In the dark, we hear the sound of a gunshot.

Lights come up on BJ looking down the barrel of a twenty-two rifle. In front of him, a distance away, is a tree with various lengths of rope hanging from its branches. Gunshot wounded bits and pieces of junk hang from the pieces of rope and surround the tree trunk—old toaster, lamp, an old wooden bingo card, newspaper clippings, a car muffler, coffee maker, washing machine etc. A hand-painted wooden sign, nailed to the tree reads: "The Hanging Tree." Another sign next to it reads: "Private Property. Trespassers Will Be Hung And Shot."

Beside the hanging tree is a large stump—JAZ's makeshift alter.

BJ cocks his rifle and shoots again. Gunshot sounds again. Lights fade on BJ and come up on the family home.

The living room looks lived-in. A comfy-looking couch, a recliner (or not), a TV set, a table lamp. Framed family photos sit here and there. A couple of abstract paintings (with recognisable Native-motif) hang on the walls.

Directly across from JAZ's stump, in a quiet corner of the living room, is MARY's altar. On it sit: candles, a cross, a Bible, a photo of the Virgin Mary.

Just behind the living room, is the family dining room. It consists of a table, four chairs and an antique desk with drawer.

The hospital room now becomes LOIS's bedroom. LOIS lies in the same hospital bed—an IV in her hand. There is no heart machine and no respirator as in Act One. Beside her bed is a small table, chair and dresser. A cross hangs above her bed.

MARY is in LOIS's room, washing LOIS's face.

JUNIOR is on the living room couch, drinking.

JAZ is sitting on the porch. She looks in the direction of the gunshot.

FRANK is rummaging through drawers in the dining room, looking for old photo albums.

FRANK (*yelling*) Mary! Mary!

Gunshot sounds.

Shit. Junior!

Gunshot sounds again. FRANK looks in direction of gunshot and shakes his head in disgust.

JAZ walks toward BJ. FRANK marches into the living room.

(*to JUNIOR*) Where the hell are they?

JUNIOR Where the hell are what?

Gunshot sounds again. FRANK points at JUNIOR's flask.

FRANK You keep that up and you're gonna end up like your Uncle Art—six feet under.

FRANK heads for porch. He looks out porch door.

Gunshot sounds again.

Je—sus. Ch—rist. I should have chopped down that goddamn tree a long time ago.

Gunshot sounds again.

FRANK heads back to the dining room. JUNIOR remains sitting on the living room couch, drinking. Lights fade on FRANK and JUNIOR and come up on BJ, standing a distance away from the hanging tree.

JAZ stands there, watching BJ. He shoots again.

JAZ Not bad.

BJ looks up at her.

What're you hanging?

JAZ peers at the hanging tree.

BJ Mom's hospital chart.

> *BJ shoots again. JAZ sits beside him. He hands her the rifle.*

Here. Go ahead.

JAZ   I'll pass, thanks.

BJ   City girl, now eh? Probably forgot how to shoot a twenty-two, anyway.

> *BJ cocks the gun and aims. JAZ stares at him, then grabs the rifle.*

JAZ   Give me that.

> *JAZ cocks the rifle and aims.*

BJ   *(pointing)* Line up the sights on that second branch to the left. And make sure you got the butt pressed firmly against your shoulder and just kind of—

> *JAZ shoots as if she's done it a thousand times before. She fires three quick shots in a row. BJ stares at her, impressed. JAZ hands the gun back to BJ.*

JAZ   City girl, eh?

> *BJ heads for the tree. JAZ follows.*

BJ   *Wah—waaahhh!*

> *JAZ laughs.*

JAZ   *Wah—waah?* *(laughing)* Beej, you've been holding out on me.

BJ   *(peering toward the hospital chart)* Christ. There's nothin' left of it.

JAZ   I didn't know you knew Cree.

BJ   Come on, Little. Everyone knows *Wah! Waaahhh!*

> *JAZ laughs. They stand at the tree, staring at it.*

JAZ   How long do you figure Uncle Art's hanging tree has been here?

BJ   I don't know—twenty years, maybe?

JAZ   Wonder what the very first thing he hung was?

BJ   Toaster.

JAZ   A toaster?

BJ   *(laughing)* Yep. He said the damn thing never worked right
from day one. Never popped the bread when it was supposed
to. Ate burnt toast for twenty years, then all of a sudden,
one day he musta woke up on the wrong side of the bed or
something. He gets up, plops his bread in the toaster and out
comes the usual two pieces of charcoal. He starts cursin' and
swearin'—rips the toaster right out of the wall, grabs a piece
of rope, his twenty-two and marches outside. Hangs the
toaster in the tree and blows the shit out of it. *(laughs)*
Auntie Mabel said he sat there shootin' and laughin', shootin'
and laughin', like he was crazed or somethin'. After that
any time anything busted or pissed him off— *(He points at
the tree.)*

JAZ   —in the hangin' tree.

           JAZ laughs.

BJ   *(smiling)* He sure was a crazy bastard.

JAZ   Hey, remember the time Auntie Mabel lost out on winning
that thousand bucks at Bingo? She woke Uncle Art out of
a dead sleep.

BJ   Christ. Imagine. One in the mornin' and they got the
floodlights on the tree, shootin' the shit outta her bingo
card. Old Man Zelski thought someone was gettin'
murdered. Called the cops and everything.

           *They laugh harder. BJ heads for the hanging tree. JAZ
follows. Lights fade.*

           *Lights up on living room. FRANK is still looking for the
photo albums.*

           *BJ inspects what's left of the hospital chart. JAZ
rummages through the junk.*

JAZ   Wow, look at all the new stuff! Either I've been away a long
time or lots of things have been pissing you off lately.

BJ   Both.

JAZ   *(picking up an eight-track tape)* Hey! My Bee Gees tape!

BJ   It had to go, Little.

JAZ   *(incredulous)* You hung my Bee Gees tape?

BJ   Christ, you played it over and over and over.

    He does a John Travolta disco move with rifle in hand.

    "Stayin' Alive" is now… dead.

    JAZ shoves him. Lights fade on hanging tree and come up on dining room. FRANK continues to look for the photo albums. MARY exits from LOIS's room with a basin of water, looks at the dirty dishes on the dining room table and sighs. She heads for the kitchen offstage. FRANK yells after her.

FRANK Mary!

    MARY stops and turns to FRANK.

    Where the hell are they?

MARY What?

FRANK The old photo albums?

MARY In the basement.

FRANK The basement? I thought they were up here.

MARY They're on the shelf by the freezer.

FRANK Oh.

    FRANK doesn't move. MARY takes a hint.

MARY *(sighing)* I'll get them. Just give me a minute.

FRANK Thanks, honey.

    MARY exits to kitchen. Lights fade as FRANK exits to living room and JUNIOR exits to dining room table.

    Lights up on hanging tree. JAZ picks up a bullet-holed goalie stick.

JAZ   Mickey Maloney's?

BJ   Yep.

JAZ   I'm sorry I missed your last game, Beej.

BJ	Ah. Just as well. Too much blood and guts.
JAZ	Against the Pas Huskies, right?
BJ	Yep. They're all Indians, eh? Tougher'n barbed wire. Damn good hockey players, though.

BJ takes the goalie stick and inspects it.

That game was tighter'n the Harrison twins.

| JAZ | Beej! |

JAZ shakes her head in disgust. BJ smiles. He puts his ballcap on backwards and pretends to be back in the game.

BJ	So. First period. Zero-Zero. Thirty-two shots on goal. Can you believe that?
JAZ	In one period?
BJ	No lie. Man, it was a rough one. Bodies spillin' everywhere. Blood splatters, like red polka dots, all over the ice. Spud the Potato knackered this guy behind our net. Jeesuz, just flattened him, eh? They called him Little Bear. He went down like a shot moose. Good thing we were wearin' helmets. Could have been scalps everywhere.
JAZ	Not funny, Beej.
BJ	I'm just tellin' ya the way it was. Those Indians are all related, eh? Five brothers all play on one line. So, you hit one brother and you hit 'em all.
JAZ	Maybe some of them were our cousins.
BJ	What?
JAZ	Some of "those" Indians might have been related to us.

BJ gives her a look.

BJ	You want to hear my story or what?
JAZ	Carry on.
BJ	Where was I?
JAZ	The brothers.

BJ	Right. Okay, fast forward. Two minutes to go in the third period, it's tied at three-three. Spud is on a breakaway and that little shittin' Bear trips him. Right in front of the net. Everybody sees it, but the ref. They don't call a penalty. The fans are goin' crazy, booin' and yellin'. Fights are breakin' out in the stands. Spud goes after the ref. We all go after Spud. Meanwhile, the game is still goin' on cause there's been no whistle. Little Bear let's this sorry-assed wrist shot go—it hits Mickey's goalie stick and dribbles in. The light goes on. And, it's game over.
JAZ	Brutal.
BJ	Tell me about it.

BJ tosses the goalie stick into the junk around the hanging tree.

JAZ	That was the same game you were scouted?
BJ	Yep. *(pause)* Dad still hasn't forgiven me, eh.
JAZ	Well. That's Dad's trip, not yours.
BJ	*(mimicking FRANK)* "Jee-zuz Ch-rist. What's wrong with you boy? You turned down a spot with the goddamn New York Islanders. The bloody NHL! You coulda been a millionaire by now!" *(beat)* I wasn't movin' to no city… no moose huntin', no fishin', no trappin'—no nothin'.

He takes the gun from JAZ.

JAZ	Mom was so happy you decided to stay home.
BJ	Yeah.

Beat. They go silent as the reality of their mother's condition hits them.

I never wanted to play hockey, eh. I did it because it was the only time I ever heard him say: "Way to go, son." The only time I made him proud. But I hated it. I hated to fight. You know why I love the bush so much, Little? *(pause)* Because it's peaceful.

Beat. BJ looks toward family home. JUNIOR exits to porch steps.

What are we gonna do without her?

BJ puts his arm around JAZ. Lights fade.

Lights up on living room. FRANK sits in his recliner channel surfing. MARY enters with a couple of photo albums. MARY hands one album to FRANK and keeps one. They flip through them. FRANK stares at a photo and chuckles.

FRANK   *(to MARY)* This was our first apartment, eh.

MARY gets up and sits next to him, on the arm of FRANK's chair.

"The icebox." Got so bloody cold in the winter, my goddamn slippers froze to the hardwood floor. Got up one morning and took one look at you sleepin' in the dresser drawer and said that's it—we're gettin' a goddamn house. *(He looks around the house.)* Your Mom sure did fix this place up, eh. Made it a real home.

MARY   *(looking around)* Yeah.

MARY points at a photo.

When was that taken?

FRANK   *(looking at photo)* Nineteen fifty-nine. That was the very first time we ever went out together.

MARY   Blind date, eh?

FRANK   Yep. I brought the whole goddamn family along with me.

MARY laughs.

Your Auntie Mabel, Uncle Art, Gert and Bert, cousin Albert. The whole goddamn crew.

MARY   Poor Mom!

FRANK   Don't know what I was thinkin'—moral support, I guess. It was so crowded at the Legion that night you couldn't see a black cat's arsehole. *(MARY cringes.)* But in walks your mother and the whole goddamn room lit up. She was a beauty, all right.

MARY   Yeah. You're lookin' pretty dapper yourself, Dad.

       BJ and JAZ head for the house.

FRANK   Yeah. Not bad. So anyway, I was trying to keep my cool, eh? But I know I got a smile on me like a wave in a slop pail. I'm tellin' ya I felt luckier than a dog with two arseholes.

MARY   *(disgusted)* Dad!

       MARY studies the photo.

       What colour was her dress?

FRANK   Jade green. With velvet sleeves. We got up on that dance floor and never left.

MARY   I loved watching you and Mom dance.

       FRANK stares at the photo.

FRANK   I used to love dancing with her. *(He sighs, then continues almost to himself.)* I took her for a drive that night, out here to Lake Atha'papa'skow. The moon was hangin' over the lake like a big bowl of honey, stars as bright as diamonds. And the goddamn Northern lights! You should have seen 'em dance. Every colour of the goddamn rainbow shimmering across the sky. Your mother's Prairie eyes were as big as saucers, eh? You know what she called 'em?

       MARY elegantly waves her hand through the air like a ballerina.

MARY   A ballet from heaven.

FRANK   That's right. A ballet from heaven. It was a real special night, all right. Real special.

       They sit in silence studying the photograph.

       JAZ and BJ approach house. BJ sits beside JUNIOR on porch steps and carves. JAZ enters living room and overhears FRANK and MARY's conversation.

MARY   Dad?

FRANK   Yeah?

MARY   Why aren't there any pictures of your mom?

       JAZ anxiously awaits FRANK's answer.

FRANK	There just aren't any.
MARY	Not even one?
FRANK	*(suddenly cold)* I said no, didn't I? Goddamnit!

FRANK gets up and heads for LOIS's room.

MARY	*(quietly, almost to herself)* I just wondered what she looked like, that's all.

MARY watches him go. She sees JAZ. FRANK enters LOIS's room. He sits beside his wife and holds her hand.

JAZ	*(to MARY)* She was Native.

MARY ignores her. She puts the photo album down and heads for the dining room table.

Mom told me.

MARY starts to clear the table. JAZ helps her.

She met her once, you know.

MARY	If you're going to talk like a crazy person, do it outside. I don't have time for this.

They clear the table in silence.

What was he thinking—bringing her home.

JAZ	He just wants her to be comfortable.
MARY	He wants her here because he hates hospitals.
JAZ	It's more peaceful here.
MARY	Peaceful? This house has never been peaceful.
JAZ	She needs her family, Mare.
MARY	She needs the nuns. She needs a priest. If she doesn't receive the last blessing, she's going to spend eternity in purgatory! She hasn't confessed her sins, she hasn't repented, she—
JAZ	She doesn't need to—
MARY	—she needs the priest to give the last blessing for her soul's final victory.
JAZ	Why don't you bless her?

MARY	*(horrified)* How can you say such a thing?
	MARY drops a dish.
	(hysterical) I broke it! I broke her favourite dish!
JAZ	It's okay, Mare.
	JAZ starts to pick up the broken pieces. MARY helps her.
MARY	No, it's not! No, it's not. She's going to go to hell!
JAZ	You don't need a priest to walk Mom to the Other Side. We can do a ceremony together.
MARY	That's blasphemous!
JAZ	We can, Mare. We can prepare Mom in a good way for her journey to the Spirit World.
MARY	Spirit World?!
JAZ	Heaven. Spirit World. It's the same thing.
MARY	It certainly is not. *(to herself)* Jesus, have mercy. *(She crosses herself.)*
JAZ	Jesus. God. Creator. We're talking about the same spirit, Mare.
MARY	There is one God and only one God.
JAZ	They're just names. Even the Bible refers to God as Creator, Jehovah, Yo-wah, Ya-way—
MARY	*(stumped)* —Yeah, well.
JAZ	The Creator created the world, so why wouldn't he speak to us through all beings and things? The four-leggeds, the winged ones—
MARY	—Don't talk about that pagan stuff in this house.
JAZ	— the water, Grandmother Moon—
MARY	—"Thou shalt not make to thyself any graven image, nor the likeness of any thing that is in heaven above, or on the earth beneath or in the water under the earth. Thou shalt not bow down to them, nor worship them." Exodus: Chapter 20; Versus 4 to 5.

JAZ   *(quickly)* "If you would learn more, ask the cattle, seek information from the birds of the air. The creeping things of the earth will give you lessons, and the fishes of the sea will tell you all. *(pause)* Job: Chapter 12; Versus 7 to 10.

MARY   *(stunned by JAZ's knowledge of the Bible)* This is—you are— I'm not going to argue—

JAZ   I don't want to argue with you, Mare. I just want to do a ceremony with Mom.

MARY   *(patronising)* Look. We all know you're not well, okay?

JAZ   I'm fine.

MARY   But, that doesn't mean you can go around inflicting everybody with your craziness.

JAZ   I'm crazy because I want to do a ceremony with Mom?

MARY   I know about your stay in that hospital. About you seeing a shrink and all.

JAZ   You're right—years ago, I spent some time on a psych ward. For two "whole" weeks. I was depressed. Suicidal. Life didn't make sense. I met a Medicine Woman when I was there.

MARY   Another nutcase.

JAZ   She was visiting her sister. She saved my life.

MARY   *(exasperated)* Lord, give me strength.

JAZ   She told me not to be afraid of what I saw. She said the Creator had given me a gift to see over the mountain like the eagle.

MARY   *(yelling offstage)* Dad!

JAZ   Mary, I'm not crazy. They locked up a lot of our people—

MARY   "Our" people?—

JAZ   —Healers. Medicine people. Those who have the gift of visioning. How do you think I knew Mom was sick?

MARY   BJ called you—without running it by the rest of us, I might add.

JAZ	No, I knew, Mare. I called the hospital. I knew Mom was sick because she came to me. She—
MARY	*(yelling offstage)* —Dad!
JAZ	...she appeared before me and—
MARY	Quit this crazy talk right now! You need to be locked up so you can't—
JAZ	Whether you want to believe it or not, Mare. We're part Indian.
MARY	We. Are. Not. Indian!
JAZ	Dad's half. That still makes us Indian.
MARY	You're delusional.
JAZ	No, I'm Métis. *(pause)* And so are you.

MARY heads for her altar. JAZ follows her.

MARY	Hail Mary. Full of Grace. The Lord is with thee—

MARY tunes JAZ out. She counts her rosary beads and quickly recites the Hail Mary prayer over and over again as JAZ speaks. Every once in awhile, MARY connects with something JAZ says. She looks up at JAZ, then immediately looks down and goes back to her Hail Mary's.

(under JAZ) —Blessed are thou among women. Blessed is the fruit of thy womb, Jesus. Holy Mary, Mother of God, pray for us sinners now and at the hour of our death. Amen. Hail Mary full of grace...

JAZ	You don't think I'm confused about who I am? You think it's easy walking around with *one moccasin stuck in a snowshoe and one boot stuck in a city grate?* I live in an urban forest full of sirens and car alarms and drunks screaming outside my window and dream about being back in the bush. Only I come home to my *roots—to the north—*and I feel so claustrophobic I can't breathe. Everybody watching. And judging. And sneering every time I open my mouth. Home sweet home. Back to the *trap line* I grew up on. Back to *Fish Fridays and Moose Mondays* and my family pretends we're a bunch of *slightly tanned French Canadians! (pause)*

Nothing Indian about us, eh Mare? *(She ruffles MARY's hair. Mary pushes her hand away.)* We just happen to like the outdoors. Ah, the fresh air! Hunting. Trapping. Fishing. The sport of it all, right Mare!

> *JAZ sarcastically kneels beside MARY and clasps her hands in prayer to try and get MARY's attention. MARY continues to pray.*

If our family hunted for sport, how come we had to eat *moose steak, moose hamburger, moose sausage, moose loaf, moose surprise!*

> *JAZ stares at MARY, still counting her rosary. An exasperated JAZ shakes her head and stands up.*

My girlfriends made money from babysitting, not trapping animals. They didn't spend two months of their summer holidays living in a huge tent with a dirt floor and cooking stove, *fishing for pickerel every single day* until they had enough fillets for a *hundred Fish Fridays.* Their *freezers* weren't filled up with a year's supply of *wild game. Imagine!* They actually *bought* their *meat* from the *grocery store.* But, I light a little *sage* and everybody goes *crazy!*

> *MARY's prayer ends at the same time as JAZ's monologue.*

MARY It's not about you! In case you haven't noticed, our mother is dying! She needs a priest!

> *MARY starts to exit.*

JAZ A priest? Mom hasn't been to church in years!

> *MARY stops and turns to JAZ.*

MARY Because of you! Because you—

JAZ Because I what, Mare?

> *Silence.*

Go ahead! Say it. Say it!

> *A beat. They stare at each other.*

MARY	She needs a priest. "Is any man sick among you? Let him bring in the priests of the church… and the Lord shall raise him up; and if he be in sins they shall be forgiven him."
JAZ	Mom's not a sinner!
MARY	We're all sinners!
JAZ	We may need the Creator's help, but we're not sinners!
MARY	You—You're the biggest sinner of all! You'll never be forgiven for what you did!
JAZ	My Creator has forgiven me.
MARY	Your Creator. Your Creator!
JAZ	It's you who hasn't forgiven me.
MARY	YOU KILLED SOMEBODY!
JAZ	I AM NOT A MURDERER!
MARY	YOU HAD AN ABORTION!
JAZ	IT'S NOT MY FAULT YOU CAN'T HAVE KIDS!

FRANK enters and hears this.

A stunned and hurt MARY quickly exits to LOIS's room.

(calling after her) I'm sorry, Mare. I…

FRANK	*(to JAZ)* Christ, what's wrong with you?
JAZ	*(to MARY)* I didn't mean it. I… I'm sorry.

MARY enters LOIS's room. We see her change the IV bag.

FRANK	*(angrily to JAZ)* Why are you so different? Travelling all over the place. *(motions to a couple of paintings on the wall)* Painting weird stuff nobody can understand. I mean, why can't you be normal—like your brothers and sister.

JAZ grabs her fringed jacket, her Native bag and storms out in tears.

(yelling after her) Get a real job! Get married! Settle down for once! Christ!

FRANK stares after her. He shakes his head, walks over to living room, plops down in his recliner. He turns on the TV and channel surfs. Lights fade on FRANK.

Lights come up on porch steps. JUNIOR sits, drinking from his flask. BJ sits beside him, carving. As JAZ exits, JUNIOR holds up a hand—the same gesture portrayed in bad spaghetti westerns.

JUNIOR   How.

JAZ stares at him, incredulously. She starts to say something then changes her mind and walks away.

JAZ   *(mumbling to herself)* How. I'd like to know *how* I got born into this family?

JUNIOR puts his hand to his mouth and pats it— another bad spaghetti western portrayal.

JUNIOR   Whoo. Whoo. Whoo.

JAZ storms over to stump in backyard. She looks to the sky.

JAZ   *Manitou pewecihin!*

Lights fade on JAZ at stump and come up on porch steps.

BJ   *(to JUNIOR)* Why do you have to do that?

JUNIOR   Do what?

BJ   Torment her like that.

JUNIOR   Because. She's a flake. Look at her. Who in their right mind would wear a jacket like that?

BJ gets up and heads inside. JUNIOR pats his mouth again.

(after BJ) Whoo. Whoo. Whoo.

JUNIOR laughs. He attempts to pour whiskey from a 26oz bottle into his flask, but is so drunk he starts to spill it. Frustrated, he tosses the flask to the bottom of the porch steps and drinks straight from the bottle. JUNIOR gets up and heads for backyard.

MARY exits LOIS's room to dining room table. She picks up the phone and dials.

BJ enters living room. He looks at FRANK, then heads for LOIS's room. BJ overhears MARY's telephone conversation and stops.

MARY Hi, Father O'Malley? It's Mary. Mary LaFontaine. I was just wondering what time you'll be coming by today? *(pause)* Oh. Yes. Okay. Okay. I'll see you then. Thank you, Father. *(pause)* God Bless you too, Father.

She smiles, hangs up phone.

BJ When's the priest comin'?

MARY Around dinner time.

BJ nods and heads for LOIS's room. MARY exits offstage and comes right back on with one of FRANK's shirts, a needle and thread. She sits at the dining room table and sews a button on the shirt. FRANK watches television in living room. Lights fade on living room.

Lights up on JAZ in backyard. Her smudge bowl sits on the stump, burning. JAZ crouches and smudges (washes herself with the smoke, carrying it with both hands over her face, head, heart). She raises both hands to the sky, stands and faces the four directions as she prays, beginning in the east, then south, west, north.

JAZ *(slowly and clearly)* Nimanitou. Great Spirit. Grandmothers and grandfathers who sit in the four sacred directions. Father Sky. Mother Earth. This is your granddaughter, Muskiki Apocoos Iskwew. I come to you in humbleness and respect for all of your good creation.

I am small and weak and need your help. My family doesn't understand our sacred ceremonies. They're afraid, Creator. Please help us. *Nineskomon, Manitou. Ayayawes niwakomakunak. Ho.*

A drunk JUNIOR, holding a bottle of whiskey, enters backyard and watches JAZ.

BJ kisses his mother's cheek and exits to porch steps. Spotlight on BJ. He sees JUNIOR's flask. He looks around to make sure nobody is watching, then picks up the flask. He stares at the flask, then puts it in his pocket. He carves.

JAZ raises her hands skyward a second time with more desperation.

JUNIOR   Dad catches you smoking that shit and you're dead meat.

JAZ   I wasn't smokin' anything. I was smudging.

JUNIOR   I don't care if you were bongin' it or bakin' brownies with it, you know how Dad feels about weed.

JAZ   It's sage, Junior.

JUNIOR   Whatever.

JAZ   It's a sacred medicine.

JUNIOR   Yeah, sure it is. *(pause)* Who you talking to, anyway?

JAZ   I was praying.

JUNIOR   If there "was" such a thing as God—which there "isn't"— Mom wouldn't be dying right now.

JAZ   The spirit never dies, Junior.

JUNIOR   You're born. You die. End of story.

JAZ   I don't believe that's the way it is.

JUNIOR   You wanna bet?

JAZ   Great Spirit is everywhere, Junior. *(waving her arms around)* In all beings. All things—the air, the water, the earth, the tree, people—

JUNIOR   Okay, okay. Now I *know* you were smokin' pot! *(pause)* Got any more?

JAZ   Is it because of Harold Bear?

JUNIOR   Harold Bear?

JAZ   Is that why you hate Indians so much?

JUNIOR   What the hell are you talking about?

JAZ   Because he beat you up?

JUNIOR	*(laughing)* That little shit?
JAZ	I can understand how that would make you afraid, Junior. I really can.
JUNIOR	*(angry)* Harold Bear is nothin' but a welfare-chaser! I work damn hard for my money. I don't rely on the fuckin' government!
JAZ	Neither do First Nations people.
JUNIOR	I'm so sick of hearing them whine about us taking away their land! How they can't hunt, they can't fish. Jee-zus! Get a life!
JAZ	It's a little more complicated than that, Junior.
JUNIOR	You know what their problem is? They're fuckin' lazy! Want-somethin'-for-nothin' lazy bastards!
	Beat.
JAZ	What if I told you Grandma LaFontaine was a full-blood Cree?
JUNIOR	You're nuts.
JAZ	It's true, Junior. Grandma was Cree.
JUNIOR	*(sarcastic, looking at his skin)* I guess that's why we all look so Indian, then.
JAZ	It has nothing to do with the colour of your skin.
JUNIOR	Oh, no? How many white Indians do you see walking around? *(He laughs.)*
	FRANK exits to LOIS's bedside. BJ exits porch steps to living room. He continues to carve.
JAZ	Actually, I know a lot of Métis people with blond hair and blue eyes. Being Native has nothing to do with how dark your skin is—it's about the medicine you carry in here. *(She pats her heart.)*
JUNIOR	For chrissakes! First, you're a Born-Againer. Then you're a Buddhist. Now, you're a wannabe Injun. What's your problem, anyway?
	JUNIOR drinks. JAZ watches him.

JAZ   I'm not the one with the problem.

JUNIOR   Did your umbilical cord get wrapped around your neck on
             your way out? Christ!

             *JUNIOR storms back to the porch steps. JAZ watches him
             go. Lights fade on JAZ.*

             *Lights come up on MARY at the dining room table,
             sewing a button on one of FRANK's shirts. She picks up
             the shirt and heads for LOIS's bedroom. She sees that
             FRANK is with her mom, and heads for the living room
             couch. BJ sits on the couch, carving. MARY sits beside
             him and sews.*

             Lights fade on living room and come up on LOIS's room.

FRANK   You comfortable, honey?

             FRANK fluffs her pillow.

             There you go. *(He stares at her and takes her hand in his.)*
             I… I don't know what to say to these kids of ours. *(pause)*
             Jesus, how did the six of us make it in this house, anyway?
             (pause) Told you we'd go to Europe when it was paid for,
             but—I'm sorry, honey. I know how much you wanted to
             see Paris. Next year, I said. Next year. And now… *(He cries.)*
             If I had the chance to do it over again, I'd take you around
             the goddamn world. We'd stop and have a dance in every
             country, eh honey? *(pause, strokes her head)* Sure made 'em
             stare when we were on the dance floor, eh Lo?

             FRANK sings "You are My Sunshine."

             (singing) "You are my sunshine, my only sunshine.
             You make my happy when skies are grey.
             You'll never know dear, how much I love you.
             Please don't take my sunshine away."

             *Lights up on porch steps. JUNIOR continues drinking
             whiskey straight from the bottle. He is quite drunk. It is
             getting dark. An owl hoots.*

             *FRANK continues to sing under JUNIOR, as JUNIOR
             freaks out on a hooting owl.*

"The other night, dear as I lay sleeping
I dreamt I held you in my arms,
When I awoke dear, I was mistaken
So I hung my head and I cried.

You are my sunshine, my only sunshine.
You make my happy when skies are grey.
You'll never know dear, how much I love you.
Please don't take my sunshine away."

JUNIOR   Shut up you stupid, bird. *(another hoot)* I said SHUT THE FUCK UP! Where's BJ and his bloody rifle when you need him? *(He drinks from his bottle, then pretends to shoot the owl with an imaginary gun.)* Fuck. *(pause)* Fuck, fuck, fuck!

> *Lights fade on JUNIOR and come up on MARY and BJ sitting in living room. BJ carves. (NOTE: BJ's carving is taking the shape of a fox.) MARY looks toward front porch.*

MARY   I'm worried about Junior. *(pause)* He's been drunk for a week.

BJ   Oh, really. I hadn't noticed.

> *FRANK continues singing. He pretends to be dancing with LOIS.*

FRANK   "In all my dreams dear I see you leave me.
When I awake my poor heart pains,
So won't you come back and make me happy,
I forgive you—I take all the blame…

You are my sunshine, my only sunshine…"

MARY   Can't you talk to him?

BJ   What am I gonna say?

MARY   How about: "quit drinking so much."

BJ   It's not my place, Mare. He has to come to that on his own.

MARY   He's showing absolutely no respect for Mom. Or you and Dad, for that matter.

BJ   I understand where he's at.

MARY   Well, if you can quit, why can't he?

BJ   Maybe he will one day. Maybe he will.

            Lights fade on MARY and BJ and come up on JUNIOR
            sitting on porch steps. He guzzles whiskey straight from
            the bottle. Lights fade on JUNIOR and come up on
            FRANK, still singing and dancing.

FRANK   "… you make me happy when skies are grey.
            You'll never know dear *(voice cracking)*
            …how… much… I… love you…"

            He looks at his empty arms and breaks down, crying. He
            goes to LOIS and cries, his head on her chest.

            BJ exits living room and heads for LOIS's room.

            (through tears) I… I hope you know how much I love you,
            Lo. I… I should've told you more often. I should have—
            (pause) I'm the one who should be lying there. Not you.
            God, not you. You never hurt a soul in your life. *(pause)*

            BJ stands in doorway and listens to his father speak.

            All those years I was drinking—I'm sorry, honey. I'm sorry.
            I'm so sorry…

            FRANK sobs.

BJ   You're sorry!? Now, you're sorry?! You treated her like shit!

            FRANK turns and sees BJ. He's angry and embarrassed
            BJ has seen this vulnerable moment.

FRANK   What are you doing here? Get out! Get out of here!

BJ   She didn't deserve your bullshit! She didn't deserve to be
            treated like that—

FRANK   Watch your mouth!

BJ   —You treated us all like shit! And now, you think gettin' all
            sentimental is gonna to make up for it—

FRANK   —Get out of here you son-of-a-bitch!

BJ   —Well, it's too late! You're too late old man!

            FRANK loses it.

FRANK	You—you good for nothin' little shit! After all I've done for you!
BJ	All you've done for me? Am I supposed to thank you for beating the shit out of me every single day of my life! For—
FRANK	—all the hockey equipment!—
BJ	—for making Mom cry herself to sleep!—
FRANK	—driving you to the rink at six in the mornin'!—
BJ	—for scaring the shit outta everybody with that bloody belt of yours!—
FRANK	—and you quit! You're a quitter!—
BJ	— you—you killed her! It's your fault she's dying!

> *FRANK lunges at BJ. He grabs BJ and hits him. BJ falls to the floor. He touches his face where FRANK hit him. He stares at his father.*

You bastard. I'm never gonna let you near my kids! You hear me?!

> *BJ storms out to living room. FRANK stares after him. He starts to shake. For the first time in his life, FRANK truly sees himself—the way he used to act when he was drinking. He turns and looks at his wife. He lies down on the bed beside her, curls up like a child and lays his head on her chest.*

> *Lights up on living room. As BJ enters, MARY who has overheard the fight, fidgets uncomfortably. She goes to BJ. He shakes her off and angrily exits outside to porch steps. BJ picks up a chair on the porch and throws it as hard as he can.*

FU-UCK! *(in FRANK's direction)* FUCK YOU!

> *BJ storms around. JUNIOR watches him. BJ lights a cigarette. Lights fade on porch and come up on LOIS's room.*

> *MARY enters LOIS's room. She goes to her father.*

MARY	Come on, Dad. It's okay. Come on. Everybody's a little tense right now.

> *MARY tries to get him up. He doesn't move. He holds onto his wife and cries.*

We're going to be okay.

> *MARY gently takes his arm and tries to get him up. He isn't going anywhere. She gives up.*

You hungry?

> *FRANK doesn't respond.*

You gotta eat something, Dad. Your blood sugar is going to go crazy. *(pause, stares at him)* I'll make some sandwiches.

> *She nervously exits offstage to kitchen. Lights fade on FRANK. Lights come up on porch. BJ has a red welt on his face. He paces, trying to calm down. A drunk JUNIOR drinks from his bottle and watches BJ.*

JUNIOR   Five fuckin' days of the same shit. Sittin' around waitin' for her to—She can't even breathe for chrissakes!

> *JUNIOR drinks.*

This is fuckin' bullshit!

> *BJ doesn't respond. BJ eyes bottle of whiskey, longingly.*

BJ   If you want to see Mom, I'd suggest you do it now.

JUNIOR   I don't need to see her like that!

BJ   She doesn't have long, Junior.

JUNIOR   *(slurring)* That woman in there with tubes shoved up her nose is not my mother! All right? My mother's beautiful. *(pause)* Do you hear me? *(quietly)* She's beautiful.

> *JUNIOR drinks.*

BJ   I know this is hard, Junior, but I just thought that if you wanted to see her—Mare called the priest.

JUNIOR   I wish she'd just get it over with and die!

BJ   Shut up! You just shut up!

JUNIOR   Look who's telling who to shut up? Christ. You don't hear me goin' on and fuckin' on. Tellin' the same boring fishing story a thousand times.

BJ	No. We get the pleasure of hearing you go on and on about your stupid stock market!
JUNIOR	At least I can afford to buy my meat at a grocery store! I don't have to shoot it!

> *BJ starts to exit.*

You tryin' to be an Injun, like Poca-fuckin'-hontas, there?

> *BJ stops. He turns and points his finger at JUNIOR.*

BJ	Don't push me, Junior!

> *BJ stares at him.*
>
> *FRANK gets up from LOIS's side and exits to living room.*

JUNIOR	Here, have a drink! *(holds out his bottle)* Oh, right. You don't drink anymore. Too bad. *(JUNIOR drinks.)* Can't hold down a job. Can't drink.
BJ	You've got a big mouth, you know that? And I'm sick of hearing it flap and flap and flap like a goddamn wounded goose. How many times did it get you into trouble in the schoolyard, eh? I should have let those kids kick your ass instead of fighting your battles for you.

> *FRANK enters living room and overhears the fight.*

FRANK	*(under his breath)* Jesus Christ. What now?

> *He heads for porch to break up fight.*

JUNIOR	I never asked for your help.

> *FRANK is about to open the door when he hears BJ say…*

BJ	Do you know what brand his belt was, Junior?
JUNIOR	*(confused)* What?
BJ	*(yelling toward house)* What was it, Dad? Western Leather. Size 36. One and a half inch width. How would I know that, eh Dad?

> *Unbeknownst to BJ and JUNIOR, FRANK stands at the door, paralysed.*

JUNIOR   For fuck sakes. It was years ago, okay? Why can't you just let it go?

> *FRANK retreats back to the living room.*
>
> *BJ and JUNIOR stand off.*

BJ   Let it go? Let it go?! You never got hit for not being able to tie your shoelaces, did you? You never got the shit beat out of ya for gettin' your fishin' line tangled! No, no you didn't, Junior. That's because you're Daddy's little boy. Isn't that right? Can't do anything wrong in Daddy's eyes, can you?

> *FRANK sits down in his recliner and stares at TV numbly.*

JUNIOR   Fuck you!

> *BJ grabs him. JUNIOR doesn't fight back. He is passive, arms hanging by his sides. BJ makes a fist and pulls his arm back. He is about to punch JUNIOR, but stops. He can't do it. He starts to shake.*

Hit me! Come on! Hit me! Please! Please fuckin' hit me!

> *BJ slowly lowers his fist.*
>
> *MARY rushes into living room from kitchen.*

MARY   What the heck is going on?

> *She stares out the window.*

Dad? Dad! Aren't you going to do something?

> *FRANK doesn't respond. MARY exits to porch to try and do something. She stands there, speechless.*

BJ   *(quietly)* He never hit you once. Not once.

JUNIOR   I wish he would have, okay! I wish he goddamn would have! You think it was easy for me?! You think it was easy watching him beat the shit outta you like that? I wanted him to hit me. I prayed to God every night. I prayed that he'd make him stop! I prayed that he'd hit me instead of you! *(getting choked up)* Only I found out there is no God. I'm fuckin' sorry, okay? I'm fuckin' sorry he beat you like that! My whole life I've tried to make it up to you! Fuck! I'm sorry, okay!

>*They stare at each other. BJ fights back tears, turns and walks away from JUNIOR.*

Beej!

>*BJ keeps walking. He heads toward the hanging tree.*

Beej!

>*JUNIOR sits on porch steps. He tries to fight back his tears, but can't.*

>*MARY sits down beside JUNIOR, and puts her arm around him. JUNIOR rests his head on her shoulder and cries.*

>*BJ passes by JAZ, sitting on her blanket in the backyard.*

JAZ   Beej? You okay?

>*He motions her not to follow. JAZ watches him go. Lights fade on JAZ and come up on porch steps.*

MARY   Come on, Junior. Let's go inside.

>*JUNIOR cries. He speaks in broken sentences, barely able to get the words out.*

JUNIOR   *(through tears)* Every time Dad bought me something, I'd say "Did you get Beej one?" If he didn't, I'd give him mine. Every time Dad asked me to go fishing, I'd say: "Let's pick up Beej." I tried, Mare. I tried to make it right.

MARY   I know, Junior. I know.

>*MARY helps JUNIOR inside. FRANK doesn't look up. He continues to stare at television. MARY looks at him, sadly, then exits to kitchen.*

>*JUNIOR sits down on the couch. He looks toward his father.*

JUNIOR   He's a good guy, you know.

>*FRANK doesn't respond. JUNIOR gets up and heads toward LOIS's room. He attempts to enter, but can't bring himself to do it. Beat. He turns and staggers into the living room, slumps into the couch and passes out.*

Lights come up on BJ sitting on a log at the hanging tree. An owl hoots. BJ pulls out JUNIOR's flask from his pocket and stares at it. He opens the lid, inhales deeply. He raises the flask to his lips, then stops. He stares at the flask again. He raises it to his lips one more time and stops. He stares at flask. Beat. He angrily throws it into the bushes. BJ holds his head in his hands and cries.

Lights fade on BJ and come up on JAZ in the backyard, praying. The owl hoots again. She looks in the direction of the owl.

JAZ   *(to herself)* It won't be long, now, Mom.

Lights fade on living room. FRANK numbly watches TV. JUNIOR is passed out. MARY enters from kitchen with tray of sandwiches, veggies and coffee and heads toward dining room.

MARY   *(to FRANK)* Come on, Dad. Come have something to eat. Corned beef on rye. Shaved ham on whole wheat.

FRANK exits to dining room table. JAZ enters house and heads for LOIS's room.

(pointing) These two are for you, Dad. And I don't want to hear you complaining because I didn't put mayo on them. You shouldn't be eating that stuff. And eat that broccoli. You don't eat enough vegetables.

FRANK   Thank you, Hitler.

MARY   Well, you're going to have to learn to take better care of yourself, now that Mom— *(pause)*

MARY heads to living room. She gently shakes a passed out JUNIOR.

Junior, wake up. *(pause)* Come on, Junior. You should eat something.

JUNIOR grunts and keeps sleeping. FRANK stares at him. MARY gives up and returns to dining room.

FRANK   *(rubbing his neck)* Goddamn neck has as many knots as a bloody pine tree. Givin' me a goddamn headache the size of New York.

> *MARY rubs FRANK's neck.*

FRANK Ow!

MARY Oh, Dad, I hardly touched you.

FRANK Goddamn strong hands you have. You should have become a masseuse.

> *MARY mouths FRANK's words as he says them. She has heard this same compliment for thirty years.*

MARY *(mouthing her dad's words)* "…strong hands you have. You should have become a masseuse."

FRANK Remember the pocket full of change?

MARY *(mimics her father)* "Okay, who's gonna rub my neck? All the change in my pocket or two one dollar bills?"

FRANK You always went for the change.

MARY No, I didn't. That was Jaz.

FRANK I thought it was you.

MARY *(indignant)* I was never a gambler.

FRANK Are you sure? Christ, what the hell's wrong with me. I'm losin' my goddamn mind.

MARY We're all a little stressed.

> *Heavy silence. MARY stops massaging FRANK's neck. She sits.*

FRANK Bet this is the first time all you kids have been home together in what?

MARY A long time Dad.

FRANK Christ, kids grow up fast. It seems like just yesterday you guys were standin' over there gettin' measured.

> *FRANK points to a wall with his lips. MARY looks.*

Look at all those goddamn pencil marks on the wall. Your mother wouldn't let me paint over them, eh? No goddamn way. *(he laughs)* Jeezus Christ. *(pause)* She sure loves you kids. Been a goddamn good mother to you.

MARY   *(choking back tears)* Yeah. She sure has, Dad.

                FRANK puts his hand on hers.

                As lights fade on MARY and FRANK, we hear the owl hoot. It is night. Show passage of time—lights come up on family members, one at a time.

                BJ leaves hanging tree and heads for the house. He stares at the outside door. Reluctantly, he enters living room. They all look at him, relieved. BJ heads straight for LOIS's room. Nobody knows what to do. This is the first time they've seen him since the fight with FRANK.

                BJ enters LOIS's Room. JAZ looks up at him. She kisses her mother on the cheek, then starts to exit. She gives BJ a hug on her way out. BJ sits beside his mother. He strokes her head.

                JAZ enters the house. She passes by FRANK and MARY in the dining room. Awkward moment. She continues into the living room and sits beside JUNIOR on the couch.

                JUNIOR, who has been passed out on the couch, comes to. He looks at JAZ and yawns and does a "whoo whoo whoo." He heads for the kitchen.

JUNIOR   *(passing by FRANK)* You want a diet coke, Dad?

                FRANK shakes his head, no.

                LOIS fidgets. BJ exits to living room. FRANK stares at him. FRANK exits to LOIS's bedside.

                JAZ sits in living room, flipping through a photo album.

BJ   *(to MARY)* I think Mom's in pain. She was fidgeting when I was in there.

                JUNIOR enters from kitchen with glass of coke and hears this.

JUNIOR   *(entering)* She needs more morphine.

                MARY sighs, exasperated. She gets up. JAZ jumps up.

JAZ   *(heading for LOIS's bed)* It's okay, Mare. I can do it.

MARY	No, I'll do it.
JAZ	I don't mind, Mare.
MARY	I said I'd take care of it.
JUNIOR	Somebody do it for chrissakes!
MARY	Look, I'm the one who knows what's going on around here.
JAZ	I just want to help.
JUNIOR	Would somebody get her some more fuckin' morphine!

> *As MARY speaks throughout this scene, the characters interject with overlapping dialogue.*
>
> *JUNIOR pours some rye into his glass of coke.*

MARY	You want to help? Now, you want to help! You haven't helped in ten years.
JAZ	Just because I haven't been home, doesn't mean I don't care.
MARY	You've caused Mom a lot of grief, you know that?
BJ	Come on, Mare.
MARY	*(angry)* Living here. Living there. Starving artist. No money. Mom has worried about you constantly.

> *A smiling JUNIOR sits back, crosses his arms like he's at an event.*

JAZ	No, she hasn't.
MARY	It's time you grew up!
JAZ	I have grown up!
MARY	You've always been Mommy's little girl!
JAZ	I can't help it if I was born last.
MARY	That's not what I'm talking about and you know it.
BJ	Come on, you guys.
JAZ	What are you talking about?
MARY	Mom has always doted on you.
JAZ	No, she hasn't.

MARY	You don't even know how to cook a meal, for goodness sake.
BJ	I don't think now is a good—

BJ gives up and sits back down.

JAZ	I cook for friends all the time.
MARY	Oh, really. I suppose you even do your own laundry, now. How big of you.
JAZ	What's wrong, Mare?
MARY	I know she still sends you money.
BJ	*(to MARY)* Mare, she buys us all stuff.
MARY	I'm not talking about gifts, BJ. I'm talking about Mom supporting Jaz cause she can't stand on her own two feet.
JAZ	I've supported myself for years.
MARY	That's a lie.
JAZ	I have, Mare.
BJ	Please, you guys.
MARY	Let me tell you something little Miss Haven't Been Home in Ten Years! You—
JAZ	It's not like I live a few hundred miles away and can just hop on a bus and come home.
JUNIOR	*(to JAZ)* You didn't even come home when Dad had his heart attack.
BJ	Stay out of it, Junior.
JAZ	Mom told me not to. And, I called. I called every day.
JUNIOR	*(to JAZ)* You should've come home. Mare's right. Mom always protects you.
BJ	*(to JUNIOR)* Don't start, okay?
JUNIOR	*(to BJ)* She's the one who started it.
MARY	*(quickly)* Where were you when Mom broke her arm? When Auntie Mabel died? When Mom retired? When the house needed painting? The steps needed fixing? For birthdays? Christmas? Anniversaries? Not here, were you?

	Silence.
JAZ	*(humbly)* No. No I wasn't. I'm sorry.
MARY	Well, it's a little late for that, isn't it?
BJ	Okay, that's enough, Mare.
	MARY starts to exit, then changes her mind. She stops and turns to JAZ.
MARY	*(to JAZ)* You didn't ask to be born last? Well, I didn't ask to be born first, okay? I didn't ask to be Mom and Dad's guinea pig. I didn't ask to—
JAZ	I was just trying to help out.
MARY	— babysit the rest of you instead of going on dates. I didn't ask to—
JAZ	Let's just drop it.
JUNIOR	For chrissakes, is anybody gonna get the fuckin' morphine?!
BJ	*(to JUNIOR)* Why don't you do it, Junior. You haven't been in to see Mom since she got sick.
JUNIOR	*(to BJ)* Fuck you!
BJ	*(to JUNIOR)* No. Fuck you, Junior. Fuck you!
MARY	*(breaking down)* —be the responsible one. Why was I the one who had to get dinner ready for you guys when Mom—
JAZ	—I was too young to cook.
	FRANK hears the fight from LOIS's room. He looks toward living room and shakes his head in exasperation.
MARY	—was at work. I didn't ask to help you with your homework, get you dressed, get you to school on time!—
JUNIOR	*(to MARY)*— Nobody fuckin' dressed me!—
MARY	—I didn't ask to be the one to protect you when Dad was drunk. I didn't ask to be the one not allowed to feel. To be the strong—
JUNIOR	—For fuck sakes! We get it okay.
MARY	—one. To be the one everybody dumps on!

> *FRANK looks in direction of all the yelling. He starts to exit LOIS's room.*

JUNIOR *(to MARY)* You do the martyr thing all by yourself.

BJ *(stands)* Give it a rest, Junior.

MARY I didn't ask to be in charge of this nightmare!

JUNIOR *(stands)* SOMEBODY GET HER SOME MORE FUCKIN' MORPHINE!!

> *FRANK enters. They all sit at once. FRANK stares at his children.*

FRANK *(quietly)* You don't think she can hear? Eh? Let me tell you something—she can hear every goddamn word you're sayin'.

> *FRANK exits to porch steps. He sits and looks up at the sky.*
>
> *MARY exits to LOIS's bedside and injects morphine into her.*
>
> *Living room. JUNIOR drinks. BJ carves furiously.*
>
> *JAZ exits to porch steps. FRANK looks up at her, then back at the sky. He moves over to make room for JAZ. JAZ sits beside him. They stare at the stars in silence. Throughout this scene father and daughter don't have eye contact.*
>
> *BJ exits out side door to hanging tree. Lights fade on living room and come up on porch steps.*
>
> *JAZ and FRANK continue to stare at the sky. We hear loons, crickets.*

JAZ Beautiful night, eh?

> *Silence.*

I forgot how still the nights are. *(pause)* How alive the air is.

> *She inhales deeply. Silence. They continue to stare at the sky.*

Dad. Look! *(points to sky)*

FRANK Well, I'll be goddamned!

Colourful lights fill the sky—blue, green, pink, purple. Father and daughter are bathed in their magic. They watch the Northern Lights in silence, awestruck.

Beat.

As they stare at the Northern Lights, we see BJ take out his wood and carve. It's starting to take the shape of an animal.

MARY exits from LOIS's Room. She looks at a passed out JUNIOR, sighs then sits at dining room table.

This is a very tender scene between FRANK and JAZ. Lots of pauses, silence between sentences. They don't look at each other, unless noted. It's the sky that connects them.

FRANK   A ballet from heaven.

JAZ   Wawatay.

FRANK   Wha—what?

JAZ   Wawatay. Northern Lights in Cree.

FRANK knows what it means, but is surprised his daughter knows Cree. He takes this in. They continue to look at the light show.

I've never seen them so bright. Wow. Look at that! You ever seen them turn purple like that?

FRANK   After forty years livin' up north, you seen it all.

Beat.

JAZ   *(pointing)* Wow! Did you see that!

FRANK   *(looking)* What?

JAZ   Shooting star.

FRANK   Missed it.

JAZ   *(pointing again)* Another one!

FRANK   Where?

JAZ   *(pointing again)* Dad! There!

FRANK	Where in hell are you lookin'?
JAZ	*(pointing again)* Look!
FRANK	*(pointing)* Well, I'll be goddamned! I saw that bastard. How many is that?
JAZ	Four.
FRANK	Well, Jeezus Christ. Guess I haven't seen everything. Never seen four shootin' stars in one night and you see 'em in ten seconds. Jesus, that's something, eh?
JAZ	Yeah, that's something, Dad. *(pause)* Four is a powerful number in First Na—
FRANK	What's that?
JAZ	Uh… nothing.

> Beat.

FRANK	Did ya make a wish?
JAZ	*(still looking at the sky)* Yeah.
FRANK	You know what I wish?
JAZ	What's that?
FRANK	I wish I'd sat on this porch watchin' the Northern Lights with you twenty years ago.
JAZ	Yeah.
FRANK	Yeah. *(pause)* Yeah.

> Beat. They continue to look up at the sky.

JAZ	She's going to go tonight, Dad.

> FRANK looks at her for the first time during this scene. JAZ keeps looking at the Northern Lights.

(pointing to the sky) Wawatay. They're calling her home. *(pause, then quietly)* The Old Ones have come to take Mom home.

> Beat. FRANK looks back at the Northern Lights.

FRANK	I want to be there with her when she—

JAZ	You will be.

> *FRANK nods. They continue to stare at the sky.*

Dad?

FRANK	Yeah.
JAZ	I… well… I want to smudge her. *(pause)* Sing her some songs. *(pause)* I want to sing Mom to the Other Side in a good way.

> *Long silence.*

FRANK	Do what you need to do.
JAZ	*(surprised)* Okay. *(pause)* Okay.

> *JAZ starts to head inside. She stops, places her hand on FRANK's shoulder. He continues to look at the sky. JAZ enters the house. She stares at JUNIOR passed out on the couch. She covers him with a blanket.*

> *BJ walks up the porch steps where FRANK is still sitting. They don't look at each other. BJ walks past FRANK and starts to open the door. He stops, turns to say something to his father, then changes his mind and starts to enter the house. FRANK turns to say something to BJ, but can't find the words.*

> *JAZ picks up her Native bag as BJ enters house.*

> *JAZ exits to LOIS's room. BJ sits with MARY at dining room table and carves. MARY looks up from her knitting and watches JAZ go.*

MARY	*(to BJ)* She hears voices, you know.

> *BJ continues to carve.*

BJ	Mom?
MARY	No, not Mom. *Your* sister.
BJ	Oh.
MARY	Oh? That's it.

> *Lights up on LOIS's room. JAZ strokes her mother's head.*

*As she talks to her mother, JAZ pulls her Native-print
blanket out of the bag and places it on her mother. Then
she unpacks her medicines and puts them on the blanket:
an abalone shell, a small leather pouch of dried herbs, an
eagle feather. She places the herbs in the shell and lights
the smudge. She stands and holds the burning smudge
in front of her and fans the smoke in the four directions,
beginning in the east, south, west, north, then to the earth
and finally the sky.*

JAZ   It's going to be okay, Mom. Everything's going to be okay.
(choking back tears) I'm going to sing you some songs. To
carry you to the Other Side in a good way. When you hear
me singing them again, I want you to come sit with me in
the Sweat Lodge, okay Mom? *(crying)* You've been my best
friend. The only one who's ever really understood me.
(pause) It's time, Mom. You can go in peace. We'll be okay,
I promise. Don't be afraid. I'm right here. I'm right here.
Kisakgihitin. Kisakgihitin. I love you, Mom.

    *Lights up on dining room table. MARY knits. BJ sands
his carving with a piece of sandpaper. MARY looks in the
direction of LOIS's room.*

MARY   *(to BJ)* I think she should be locked up.

BJ   Mare.

MARY   She told me she has *"visions."*

BJ   What kind of visions?

MARY   What do you mean what kind of visions—she *sees* stuff that's
not real.

BJ   How do you know it's not real?

MARY   Maybe we should lock both of you up.

BJ   I'm serious, Mare. Maybe she does see stuff.

MARY   Not you too.

BJ   This old Indian guy? I met him out on the trapline, eh?
Anyway. He sees stuff.

    MARY stares at him in disbelief.

BJ   Some Indians are like that, you know.

MARY   We. Are. Not. Indian.

BJ   We're part.

MARY   Is she brainwashing you?

>   *As BJ and MARY talk, JAZ smudges herself, then her mother. She fans the smoke over her mother's body from head to toe.*

BJ   Ever see the movie "Thunderheart"?

MARY   BillyJoe!

BJ   Val Kilmer's in it.

>   *BJ elbows MARY in jest, knowing she's got a crush on Val Kilmer. She turns away in embarrassment.*

Anyway, he's got an ounce of Indian in 'im or somethin'. He looks white and everything, but his dad who's dead, you find that out as the story goes on, turns out his old man was a half-breed or somethin'. Anyway, Val Kilmer he has these visions—sort of like seein' a mirage out in the desert, is the best way to describe it. You know, kind of like he's havin' a dream or somethin' only he's awake when it happens. Anyway, he sees old Indians, hears drummin'—stuff like that. Who's to say people don't see stuff is all I'm sayin'.

>   *MARY continues to stare at him in disbelief.*

MARY   BJ! You're talking about a Hollywood movie. That hardly compares to our—*your* sister. She spent time on a psych ward. With other crazies. She was telling me she can see over the mountain… like an eagle. I mean, for the love of God, I've never heard such crazy talk.

>   *BJ laughs.*

This is not funny. I seriously think she needs to be committed. Put somewhere where she can't hurt herself or others.

BJ   Mare. She's fine. In fact, I think she's doin' better than ever. She seems to have finally found what she's been searching for all these years.

MARY	You always do this.
BJ	Do what?
MARY	Stick up for her.
BJ	She's a good kid, Mare.
MARY	You and Mom. You're both blind as bats when it comes to Jaz.
BJ	So, she's a little different.
MARY	A *"little"* different?
BJ	Got her own views and stuff. But, so do the rest of us.
MARY	We don't go around talking to the dead.
BJ	No. But some of the people we do talk to might as well be. Take Squirrely Jackson, for example. Not much upstairs if you know what I mean.
MARY	BillyJoe, this is a serious matter. I really think *your* sister is delusional.
BJ	She's your sister, too. And she's fine.

JAZ places the burning smudge on the blanket, then picks up her drum and sings in Cree: "Wawatay" ("Northern Lights" translation on page 102).

JAZ	Manitouwak nimihitowak kiya kici
	acahkosak kisikook
	Hey ya Hey ya Hey yo
	manitouwak tepwatcic kici kiya
	Hey ya Hey ya Hey yo
	niya wicewik, nikawiy pimiya
	Hey ya Hey yo
	Wawatay, mihkwaw, askihtawaw ekwa sipihkwaw
	Wawatay kipinatikawin
	Wawatay kiskosi kimanitou nikamowin
	Wawatay pimohtaha nikawiy kiwetah

Lights up on dining room table. MARY sniffs the air.

MARY	What's that smell? *(standing)* Something's on fire!

> *MARY and BJ both sniff the air, trying to figure out where the smell is coming from. They look toward LOIS's room. MARY dashes in. BJ follows her.*

(to JAZ) What's on fire?!

BJ   Oh, oh.

> *JAZ jumps. She stops chanting.*

MARY   Oh my God! Are you trying to kill her! Get this *(pointing at JAZ's medicines)* …this stuff out of here. Right now!

JAZ   Mare, please. It's just a smudge.

> *MARY starts waving the smoke away.*

MARY   Jesus, have mercy.

> *MARY crosses herself.*

BJ, quick! Make the smoke go away! Father O'Malley could show up any minute!

BJ   Calm down, Mare. It'll be okay.

> *BJ helps MARY fan the smoke away. JAZ gathers up her drum, her medicines.*

MARY   *(to JAZ)* I should have never let you alone with her! If I'd known you were going to pull a stunt like this— *(getting hysterical)* You and your pagan smoke! *"You're"* keeping the priest away!

BJ   Easy, Mare.

> *MARY makes the sign of the cross.*

MARY   *(to JAZ)* She's got to be blessed! Do you hear, me? She's got to be blessed! I want to see her again. I want to see Mom in Heaven!

BJ   Mare.

MARY   *(to JAZ)* If Father O'Malley doesn't make it in time—I'll—I'll never forgive you. I will never forgive you as long as I live!

> *JAZ takes her medicine bag, the burning abalone shell and exits to porch steps.*

Lights fade on LOIS's room and stay on JAZ. She opens the outside door just as FRANK is entering the house. FRANK stares at the smudge, then at JAZ. He nods at her. JAZ exits to backyard and places the smudge bowl on her stump and cries.

FRANK enters LOIS's room.

(to FRANK) That girl has completely lost her mind. She's trying to burn the place down! Look at all this smoke!

FRANK doesn't respond. He puts an arm around MARY and leads her out of LOIS's room. BJ sits beside his mother in silence. He holds her hand.

FRANK   Come on, honey, you're exhausted. You just need to get some sleep.

MARY picks up the phone and frantically dials.

MARY   I can't even think about sleep until Mom receives her final blessing. *(panicked)* Where is he?!

FRANK gently takes the phone from her hand and hangs it up.

FRANK   Come on, Mare. I'll come and get you when Father O'Malley gets here, okay?

MARY thinks about it.

MARY   What if he doesn't get here in time—what if—

FRANK   He's probably on his way. You go lay down.

MARY exits offstage to her bedroom, then runs back on.

MARY   Was that a car?

FRANK   What?

MARY   I thought I heard a car.

She looks out the window.

Where is he?! He should have been here by now!

She crosses to her altar in the living room and kneels. She looks up to the sky.

JAZ stands by her stump, looking up to the sky.

> MARY and JAZ scream at God/Creator together.

MARY   *(angrily to God)* Why are you doing this!

JAZ   *(angrily to Creator)* Why are you doing this!

MARY   Why?!

JAZ   Why?!

MARY   Why hasn't the priest come?!

JAZ   Why can't I send her off in a good way!

MARY   Where is he!

JAZ   All the sweats and healing circles!

MARY   I've given myself to you my whole life!

JAZ   All these medicines!

MARY   Why is this happening!

JAZ   Why is this happening!

MARY   Why goddamnit!

> JAZ and MARY sob.
>
> Lights fade on JAZ and MARY and come up on living room.
>
> FRANK heads for LOIS's room, not realising BJ is still there. Awkward moment. BJ gets up and exits past FRANK to porch steps. He looks for JAZ.
>
> FRANK sits at his wife's side. He strokes her hair. Lights fade on FRANK, who takes his wife's hand, strokes her face. Eventually we see him fall asleep.
>
> Living room. JUNIOR is still passed out on couch.
>
> Lights up on JAZ sitting on the backyard stump, crying. BJ approaches her. Northern Lights dance.

BJ   Hey, Little. How ya doin'?

JAZ   I'm okay. You?

BJ   Fine as frog's hair. *(He tousles her hair.)*

BJ gives his finished carving to JAZ. She wipes her tears and inspects the carving.

JAZ Way to go, Beej. You finished it. *(runs her hands over carving)* Fox—Keeper of the Family.

She runs her fingers over the carving. She tries to give it back, but he motions her to keep it. JAZ lifts her hands to him in gratitude.

Hy Hy.

BJ sits beside her and stares up at the Northern Lights. She picks up her drum and sings softly in Cree: "Papimohte Nikawiy" ("Walk Gently, Mom" translation on page 103).

Halfway through her song, the Northern Lights dance across the stage.

papimohte nikawiy
papimohte
waski kihci wapiskaw kisik
oti opimihk
papimohte nikawiy
papimohte
ohpina oma ekin, maka namoya nakasin

Way ya hey ya hey
Way ya hey ya heya ho

JAZ stops singing and softly drums a heartbeat rhythm, i.e., boom-boom (pause) boom-boom (pause) boom-boom...

Lights fluctuate between JAZ and FRANK, showing the passage of time. FRANK falls asleep. JAZ's drumming (heartbeat rhythm) gets slower and slower until finally, drumming stops. At the same time, MOTHER stops breathing. FRANK bolts upright. He stares at his wife. At the same time, JAZ looks toward house, then at the sky, then back at the house.

FRANK takes LOIS's hand.

FRANK *(choked up)* I love you honey. I love you.

FRANK kisses LOIS. He holds her and cries.

JAZ taps BJ.

JAZ   Beej. Mom's gone.

BJ sits up. They head for house.

FRANK exits from LOIS's room just as BJ and JAZ enter.

FRANK and JAZ share a knowing look. FRANK nods. JAZ goes to her father and embraces him. He attempts to hug her back, but feels awkward. FRANK heads for the bedroom dresser. He opens the drawer and rummages through papers.

BJ goes to MARY still kneeling at her altar. She looks up at him. He nods. MARY sobs. BJ holds her.

JAZ goes to the couch and wakes JUNIOR.

(to JUNIOR) Junior, Mom's gone.

JUNIOR quickly sits up. He looks around at everyone, then holds his head in his hands. JAZ puts her arm around him. BJ leads MARY to the living room couch. All four kids sit on the living room couch.

FRANK enters living room, holding a letter in his hand. He looks around at his family.

FRANK   A while back your mother… she told me she had written a letter. That it… it was in her drawer. She said not to open it until she…. She said that if anything were to happen to her… she… she wanted us to read this.

FRANK looks around at everybody. He chooses BJ to read the letter—a sort of peace offering. BJ takes it, breaks the seal on the envelope and pulls out a letter. He clears his throat and reads. This is the first time any of them have heard the letter, including FRANK. BJ takes in the information as he reads it out loud.

BJ   To my dear Frank, Mary, BillyJoe, Junior and Jaz:

"Many years ago, I attended a Native Healing Circle when… *(he looks at FRANK, then back at the letter)* when your Grandmother LaFontaine died. Family members came together. There were a lot of tears, but miracles happened. *(pause)* Your Grandmother… *(He clears his throat.)* '…Your Grandmother was a… a full-blood Cree…"

JUNIOR   What?

FRANK stares at him.

BJ   "You carry Métis blood."

JUNIOR   What the hell is this?

FRANK   Junior. Shut it for once. Please.

FRANK motions BJ to continue.

BJ   *(clears his throat)* "…Your grandmother was a full-blood Cree. You carry Métis blood. It's nothing to be ashamed of. Be proud of who you are. It is my dying wish that you come together as a family and heal past wounds. I want you to do this by gathering together in a… in a… traditional Healing Circle. *(pause)* Please know that wherever it is I am going after this world, I will be with you always.
Be good to each other. I love you.
Love, Mom"

A shocked silence fills the room. Everyone looks at the floor. Except JAZ. She looks at FRANK.

FRANK   Well, now you know. Your old man's a half-breed. I don't know what your mother was thinking. But, if that's her dying wish, then that's her dying wish. *(pause)* Any objections?

No one speaks. A long silence. MARY dashes from the room, to LOIS's bedside. FRANK and the others watch her go. A beat. MARY strokes her mother's face.

Jaz? You're going to have to help me out here.

JAZ   Sure, Dad.

FRANK   It's been a long time… I want you to lead the circle for me.

JAZ nods. She starts to unpack her medicines.

BJ, Junior—go get a couple of chairs from the dining room. Put them next to the couch in a circle.

BJ and JUNIOR head to the dining room to get the chairs.

Lights fade. Music up. Chanting from "Wawatay" plays. Living room lights change to red.

JAZ hands FRANK four large coloured pieces of cloth: red, yellow, dark blue and white. FRANK stares at them. A beat. He hangs them in the four directions. Red in the east. Yellow in the South. Dark blue in the West. White in the North.

As FRANK places the pieces of cloth in the four directions, JAZ puts her blanket down and unpacks her medicines: drum, drum stick, BJ's carving, her feather holder and abalone shell. She places some dried herbs in the abalone shell and lights it. She takes an eagle feather out of its holder and waves it over the smudge.

JUNIOR and BJ arrange the two chairs and couch in a semi-circle, facing the audience.

Seating arrangement, starting from L to R or clockwise: FRANK, then BJ, then empty chair for MARY, then JAZ, then JUNIOR.

FRANK sits. He motions for BJ and JUNIOR to sit.

MARY exits from LOIS's room to living room. She looks around at her family and the circle, then exits to porch steps. MARY leaves the door open a crack, so she can hear what's being said inside. MARY stands on the porch steps, next to the door for the duration of this scene. She hears everything everybody says.

JAZ smudges herself, then takes the smudge bowl and feather and walks over to FRANK, who stands. He motions for BJ and JUNIOR to stand and for BJ to take off his ball cap.

FRANK carries the smoke over his head and heart as if he's done it a thousand times. BJ and JUNIOR watch their father, in awe.

FRANK   *(holding both hands in the air) Ayayawes niwakomakunak. (translation: All my relations.)*

JAZ holds the smudge in front of BJ. BJ tries to follow his father's actions. JUNIOR feels like an idiot. He makes a face, grabs a handful of smoke throws it on himself, coughs, then waves JAZ away.

FRANK sits. He motions for BJ and JUNIOR to sit.

JAZ places the smudge on her blanket. She holds the feather in her hand.

JAZ   *(looking up)* Hy Hy, Manitou. My spirit name is Muskhikhi Apocoos Iskwew. It means Medicine Deer Woman. It was given to me by a Cree elder in a Sweat Lodge. *(She holds the feather up.)* The Eagle flies closest to the Creator. When we hold the Eagle Feather in the circle, it becomes our talking stick. It brings out the truth from the deepest places of our hearts and carries our words to Great Spirit. When you hold this feather, you speak for as long as you need to—without interruption. We'll start with Dad and go around the circle.

JAZ hands the feather to FRANK.

FRANK   *(to JAZ)* First we need a song. A Cree song. To invite our ancestors to be here with us.

JAZ nods. She places the feather on her blanket/altar and picks up her drum and stick. She is about to drum when FRANK motions for her to give him the drum.

She hands FRANK the drum. A moment passes. FRANK closes his eyes, connecting with his ancestors and begins to drum. He sings in Cree: "Miyonakosoo Niskwem" ("My Beautiful Woman" translation on page 104). The others stare in shock. JAZ gets teary.

Nimosom, nimosom, kitimakinawin
niwonisinin ekwa nipeyakon
nimosom, miyikosowin awa iskwew kiyaoci
Ewa anos etepotate otaskihk
Hey ya ho

mistahe nikaskeyihten, nicimos
kiya oma niaskiy ekwa pimacihowin
Niskwem, miyonakosoo niskwem
Tapitaw niwikimakan kiya
Hey ya ho

(Smiling, he speaks.) Bet you didn't know I had it in me?

JUNIOR You can say that again.

> *FRANK hands the drum back to JAZ. JAZ hands him the feather. He sits. The others follow his lead. FRANK strokes the feather. Beat. This is the hardest thing he's ever had to do in his life.*

FRANK It's been a long, long time since I've held an eagle feather in my hand. *(pause)* My Indian name is Amiskisis. It means "Little Beaver." It was given to me by my Kokum—my Grandmother—when I was born. *(pause)* My mother—your Kokum—married a white man—Andy McBride. My father. *(pause)* We lived on the Red Pheasant Reserve just outside of Saskatoon until I was ten. He drank too much… had a terrible temper. *(pause)* He used to beat us. Mom woke me and my brother, your uncle Art, up one night and said we were goin'. We left in the middle of the night. That was the last time I saw my father. I moved to Flin Flon when I was eighteen. To work in the mines. I met your mother when I was twenty. Two years later, my mother died. That was the healin' circle your mom talked about in her letter. I made her promise never to tell you about my family. About where I came from. It was nothing to be proud of when I was growing up. Bein' spit at. I didn't want you to have to go through what I went through. Maybe that was wrong. But, I wanted you to have a good life. *(pause)* I didn't grow up with a lot of hugs, eh. It's not easy for me to show those things. But, it don't mean I don't love you. You're good kids. *(pause)* After I quit drinkin' I didn't know where I fit anymore… you… you were all so used to goin' to your mother for everything. *(choked up, tries to get himself together)* I… I used to sit there, secretly wantin' you to come to me, you know. I just didn't know how… I didn't know how to be a father. *(He cries, then tries to collect himself. A moment.)* BJ, I know I've been hardest on you—guess you remind me too much of myself. You're a damn fine trapper. And hunter. Your Kokum would be real proud of you. She taught me how to set a trap when I was just a little fella. I want you to know I'm proud of you too, son. *(to JAZ)* And Jaz. It's good to have you home, honey. *(pause)* I know we've had our differences. I'm sorry for those things I said about getting a real job. I guess I just worry about you. Being an artist and all. Not that you're not good at what you do. Your mother and I loved gettin' your paintings in the mail. Didn't always understand them—but the colours were sure nice. *(pause)* Guess you're the one in the family who got the Indian blood the thickest, eh? Christ, you've wanted to be an Indian ever since you were little. When you kids played cowboys and Indians? You always wanted to be the Indian. Broke my heart not to tell you were one for real. Your Kokum would be real proud of you, too. *(pause)* And Junior?

JUNIOR   It's okay, Dad. You don't have to—

FRANK   Please, son. *(pause)* You're a good kid. Always been good to me. To your mother. *(pause)* There's no easy way for me to say this… you're a drunk, son. It's probably my fault—the way I drank and everything. Passed it on to you and BJ.

JUNIOR   I've got it under control, Dad.

FRANK   I don't think you do, son. I want you to know that I understand your pain. I drank for a lot of years. And I can tell you, booze don't take away that ache inside. You know, maybe the odd fishin' trip might help ease your mind a bit. You used to love huntin' and fishin'. You were happy in the bush. *(to everyone)* I wish your sister was here. But, she's got her own beliefs and that's okay. She's got a heart of gold, that one. *(pause)* She hasn't had it easy bein' the eldest. She's seen a lot. Too much. She got a bum wrap, you know. Not bein' able to have kids and all. Would've made a helluva mother. Christ knows, she's mothered the lot of you on occasion. Myself included.

> We see MARY cry.

> As FRANK speaks, LOIS gets out of bed and walks into the living room. She stands and smiles at her family. She walks behind them, pausing to place both her hands on their shoulders—one by one, she touches them. They feel her presence, but don't see her.

You kids used to be best friends. Your mother was real proud of that.

> *LOIS puts her hands on FRANK's shoulders, then moves on to BJ, JUNIOR and JAZ.*

FRANK   This ain't easy—sittin' around bein' honest. But, it's good. Been too much pain for too goddamn long. It's time we cleared the air. The past is over. We can't do anything about that. But, we're blood. Doesn't matter what goddamn colour it is either—red, blue, purple—we're family. We need to stick together. *(He raises his hands and feather to the sky.)* Ayayawes niwakomakunak.

> *LOIS begins to walk out of the living room. She stops and turns to look at her family one last time, a big smile on her face.*
>
> *FRANK hands the feather to BJ. He gives BJ's hand a loving squeeze as he hands him the feather. They lock eyes. BJ stares at the feather.*
>
> *LOIS turns and exits to front door.*
>
> *Soft, haunting music comes up.*
>
> *As BJ speaks, the lights start to fade.*

BJ   I… I *(He cries.)* I'm gonna miss her so much. She… she was a good person. A good mom… she never hurt a soul in her life…

> *As BJ talks and lights fade, LOIS opens door and exits to porch steps.*
>
> *The Northern Lights begin to dance.*
>
> *MARY looks up and sees LOIS. MARY stares at her mother in shock. LOIS touches MARY's cheek, then kisses her. She smiles, then turns and walks into the dancing Northern Lights. MARY stands and watches her mother go. We see MARY mouth the words: "Mom. Mom."*
>
> *Northern Lights get brighter and bigger, bathing the entire stage and audience in their colourful magic.*
>
> *MARY stares at the porch door. A beat. She enters the house and heads for the living room. The family all turn and look at her. JAZ moves over to make room for Mary*

on the couch. MARY sits, then hugs JAZ. They cry. BJ hands MARY the eagle feather.

FRANK, BJ, JUNIOR, MARY and JAZ look in the direction of their mother and watch her walk into the dancing Northern Lights.

The music plays on as the lights fade to black.

The Northern Lights dance in the dark.

Blackout.

The end.

Wawatay Songs

Playwright's Note: For the Firehall Arts Centre Production of Wawatay
in February 2002, only select verses of the following songs were used.
Here are the songs in their entirety. All songs are in Cree.

MUSKWA OMANITOMA	BEAR SPIRIT
Muskwa, Muskwa	Great Bear, Great Bear
kiya ki-maskawsin	You are powerful and strong
Muskwa, Muskwa	Great Bear, Great Bear
nikamo nanatawih nikamowin	Sing us your healing song
astum maskihkiy muskwa	Come Medicine Bear,
nanatawiha maskihna	and heal our wounds
astum maskihkiy muskwa	Come Medicine Bear
omanitoma masiskeweat	whose spirit soothes
Hey ya Hey yo	Hey ya Hey yo
Muskwa, Muskwa	Great Bear, Great Bear
kiya nita-masiskeweyin	Your good healing ways
Muskwa, Muskwa	Great Bear, Great Bear
ni pikiskwenan	We give you praise
astum maskihkiy muskwa	Come Medicine Bear,
nanatawiha maskihna	and heal our wounds
astum maskihkiy muskwa	Come Medicine Bear
omanitoma masiskeweat	whose spirit soothes
Hey ya Hey yo	Hey ya Hey yo

WAWATAY

Manitouwak nimihitowak kiya kici
acahkosak kisikook
Hey ya Hey ya Hey yo
manitouwak tepwatcic kici kiya
Hey ya Hey ya Hey yo
niya wicewik, nikawiy pimiya
Hey ya Hey yo

wawatay, mihkwaw, askihtawaw ekwa
     sipihkwaw
wawatay kipinatikawin
wawatay kiskosi kimanitou nikamowin
wawatay pimohtaha nikawiy kiwetah

nimihitowak Manitou aski ohci
oma ekin ohpinakahtu
wakomakunak oteoci manitouwik
manitouwak wa piskisiwak

wawatay, mihkwaw, askihtawaw ekwa
     sipihkwaw
wawatay kipinatikawin
wawatay kiskosi kimanitou nikamowin
wawatay pimohtaha nikawiy kiwetah

kimiwanis tipiskaki
nita weci-nimihtowak
taswekasta omikwanak ohpaho
neya ohpaho kihci-sokeyimo

wawatay, mihkwaw, askihtawaw ekwa
     sipihkwaw
wawatay kipinatikawin
wawatay kiskosi kimanitou nikamowin
wawatay pimohtaha nikawiy kiwetah

NORTHERN LIGHTS

Spirit Warriors are dancing for you
Across the starry sky
Spirit Warriors are calling for you
Go with them, Mom, and fly

Wawatay pink, green and blue
Wawatay have come for you
Wawatay whistle your spirit song
Wawatay, carry my mother home

A ballet from heaven,
the thin veil has been lifted
Relatives from the Other Side
Spirits so bright and vivid

Wawatay pink, green and blue
Wawatay have come for you
Wawatay whistle your spirit song
Wawatay, carry my mother home

Swirling rainbows in the night
They dance in harmony
Spread your wings, take flight
Go soar with Great Mystery

Wawatay pink, green and blue
Wawatay have come for you
Wawatay whistle your spirit song
Wawatay, carry my mother home

PAPIMOHTE NIKAWIY

papimohte nikawiy, papimohte
waski kihci wapiskaw kisik
oti opimihk
papimohte nikawiy
papimohte
ohpina oma ekin, maka namoya nakasin

Way ya hey ya hey
Way ya hey ya heya ho
nikiskeyihten namoya wahyaw e-weto
   hteyin
kawapametin kapekisik
miyahta pasu sikwan wapikwaniy
pehta kiya tepwatcik makwak
miskona maskawaw mitosak misaw
niwapaten kapapeyin anita nohkom
pisim

papimohte nikawiy, pipimohte
waski kihci wapiskaw kisik
oti opimihk
papimohte nikawiy pipimohte
ohpina oma ekin, maka namoya nakasin

Way ya hey ya hey
Way ya hey ya heya ho

nikiskeyihten namoya wahyaw e-weto-
hteyin
kawapametin kape kisik
nimiskonen kamicimineyin nipin yotin
kiwapametin ispimihk mikisiwak
   pakitinowak
namoya tapohnipayou
niweciwakun-tapweto kiya kapimatisin

papimohte nikawiy, pipimohte
waski kihci wapiskaw kisik
oti opimihk
papimohte nikawiy pipimohte
ohpina oma ekin, maka namoya nakasin

Way ya hey ya hey
Way ya hey ya heya ho

WALK GENTLY, MOM

Walk gently, Mom
Walk gently
Over the Great White Bridge
to the Other Side
Walk gently, Mom
Walk gently,
Lift the veil, but don't say goodbye.

I know you won't be far away
I'll see you in the everyday
Smell your perfume in springtime
   flowers
Hear your voice in the call of the loons
Feel your strength in cedars that tower
See your smile in Grandmother Moon.

Walk gently, Mom
Walk gently
Over the Great White Bridge
to the Other Side
Walk gently, Mom
Walk gently,
Lift the veil, but don't say goodbye

I know you won't be far away
I'll see you in the everyday
Feel your hugs in the summer wind
Watch you soar with the eagles so free
There's no such thing as the end
My friend—you will always be

Walk gently, Mom
Walk gently
Over the Great White Bridge
to the Other Side
Walk gently, Mom
Walk gently,
Lift the veil, but don't say goodbye

MIYONAKOSOO NISKWEM

Nimosom, nimosom kitimakinawin
niwonisinin ekwa nipeyakon
nimosom, miyikosowin awa iskwew
  kiyaoci
Ewa anos etepotate otaskihk
Hey ya ho

mistahe nikaskeyihten, nicimos
kiya oma niaskiy ekwa pimacihowin
Niskwem, miyonakosoo niskwem
Tapitaw niwikimakan kiya
Hey ya ho

nimosom, nipakitinowekwa omanitoma
ta-pimihat mikisiw aci ispimihk
wecihin ta-maskowcihan
wecihin kinawemin sakihtawin oci
Hey ya ho

mistahe nikaskeyihten, nicimos
kiya oma niaskiy ekwa pimacihowin
Niskwem, miyonakosoo niskwem
Tapitaw niwikimakan kiya
Hey ya ho

MY BEAUTIFUL WOMAN

Grandfather, Grandfather, please
  have pity on me
I feel so lost and alone
Grandfather, she was my gift from you
And now you have called her home

I miss you so much, my sweetheart
You were my world and my life
My woman, my beautiful woman
You will always be my wife

Grandfather, I set her spirit free
To fly with the Eagles above
Please help me to be strong
Please shelter me with your love

I miss you so much, my sweetheart
You were my world and my life
My woman, my beautiful woman
You will always be my wife